THE MAKING OF

STARSHIP TROOPERS

The Making of

STARSHIP TROOPERS

Paul M. Sammon

LITTLE, BROWN AND COMPANY

A *Little, Brown* Book

First published in Great Britain in 1997 by Little, Brown and Company
This edition reprinted by arrangement with Sony Signatures, Inc., and Boulevard Books, a member
of Penguin Putnam Inc.

Copyright © 1997 by TriStar Pictures, Inc.

The moral right of the author has been asserted.

Book design by HRoberts Design

A CIP catalogue record for this book is available from the British Library.

ISBN 0 316 64461 7

Little, Brown and Company (UK)
Brettenham House
Lancaster Place
London WC2E 7EN

CONTENTS

Acknowledgments

I would like to thank:

Paul Verhoeven: The words "focused" and "professional" have been applied so many times to Hollywood directors they've lost all currency. But if there was ever a man for whom those terms could still be coined, mint-fresh, it is Mr. Verhoeven. My appreciation to Paul-the-person as well, who keeps finding time for me no matter what the project.

Alan Marshall: For the access, info, and insights . . . not to mention the screening room jokes. Who knew that beneath the gruff exterior of this "Professional's Professional" lurked the heart of a pussycat? Or was that a mad cow?

Jon Davison: Beside whom it's been my privilege (and pleasure) to labor since 1986. During that time Jon has been unfailingly supportive, wickedly funny, and a good friend. Without him, this book simply would not be.

Ed Neumeier: Whose keen insights into the politics behind filmmaking are always appreciated. As was Ed's continued commitment to *Starship Troopers'* script—an admirable effort which helped hammer one more nail into the auteur theory's coffin lid.

Vic Armstrong: Who never said no, and has my continued respect and admiration. Here's hoping you never have to set up another plate shot, Vic . . . at least not in this century.

Then, of course, there was David Latham. Day in, day out, this indispensable *ST* contact fielded innumerable telephone calls and arranged uncountable requests, generally ensuring that my Big Bug tenure went as smoothly as possible. Enjoyed our talks, Dave!

All good things to "The Happy Girl," Stacy Lumbrezer, as well—who watched in horror as I dropped to my knees and salaamed before her desk. You were a bigger help and daily cheerer-upper than you ever realized, Stace; eternal gratitude.

Of course, *The Making of Starship Troopers* owes its very existence to the friendliness and accessibility of *ST*'s cast and crew. But since I spoke with over two hundred of you, my gratefulness will have to be shortened to a communal "thanks." May your careers continue, and your lives be full.

As for Lori Perkins, my agent—aren't you glad this isn't another *Splatterpunks*?

High hosannas to my editor at Boulevard Books, Elizabeth Beier, and to her assistant, Barry Neville, for letting me ride with the flow.

My best to Virginia Heinlein as well. I hope this effort will at least illustrate the seriousness with which the filmmakers approached your husband's work.

Penultimately, undying love to my twenty-year-plus soulmate, Sheryl Edith Sires Sammon. Was this *really* what we had in mind while lugging that typewriter to the Fine Arts?

Finally, a salute to the Grand Old Man himself, Robert Heinlein. I still well remember the "Rocket Juice" Bob lubed me with at all those conventions so many years ago. I was too young and legless to thank you then, Bob. I do so now. And wherever you are:

Rest easy, trooper.

You made a difference.

Introduction

In 1959, revered science fiction author Robert A. Heinlein published a novel destined to ignite a firestorm of controversy.

Its title? *Starship Troopers.*

Ostensibly a work of juvenile fiction aimed at a late-fifties teenage readership, *Starship Troopers* was actually a novel of ideas. Its plot may have featured giant alien insects, but Heinlein's book also celebrated the military, endorsed the use of (pragmatic) violence, and condemned liberal social programs.

Little wonder, then, that *ST* aroused strongly divided reactions at the time of its publication. Still, Heinlein's novel was a crackling good adventure story, with high-tech human soldiers waging bitter interstellar war against cunning extraterrestrial bugs. And whatever its political merits (or deficiencies), *Starship Troopers* was popular. So popular, in fact, that it has remained in print for nearly forty years.

That popularity has now prompted Hollywood to transform *Starship Troopers* into one of this century's most lavish science fiction films. Yet what's truly remarkable about this endeavor is that *ST*-the-film's creators have not only retained *Troopers'* story line, they've kept its provocative politics.

Not that there haven't been changes. *ST* director Paul Verhoeven (a controversial figure in his own right) and *ST* screenwriter/coproducer Edward Neumeier have selectively cut, retained, and expanded on the narrative found in Heinlein's novel. The *ST* filmmakers have also injected their own challenges to *Starship Troopers'* controversial concepts, while simultaneously pulling off the difficult trick of remaining faithful to the novel's core philosophy.

But such talk of concepts and philosophies obscures the fact that the cinematic version of *Starship Troopers* is, like the novel on which it is based, a large-scale entertainment. Viewers of this exciting motion picture will witness epic space battles, be touched by an emotional romance, and experience visits to exotic new worlds—all while encountering some of the most ferociously savage extraterrestrials ever created for the screen.

It is still too early to guess at how Paul Verhoeven's version of Robert Heinlein's *Starship Troopers* will be received by the public and critics. However, *The Making of Starship Troopers* will, I hope, at least testify to the sometimes painful, sometimes rewarding, always exhaustive efforts of the highly professional crew which pulled it together.

So, in the words of the ubiquitous "FedNet" announcement which appears throughout this motion picture—

Would you like to know more?

Read on . . .

— *Paul M. Sammon*
Los Angeles, CA
Summer, 1997

T

here are a dozen different ways of delivering destruction in imper-
sonal wholesale, via ships and missiles of one sort or another, catastrophes
so widespread, so unselective, that the war is over because that nation or
planet has ceased to exist. What we do is entirely different. We make war
as personal as a punch in the nose . . .

—from *Starship Troopers*
by Robert A. Heinlein

DEVELOPMENT

The Author

Like most popular art, the novel *Starship Troopers* was a child of its

times. First published in 1959, when America was beginning to shift away

from the conservative Eisenhower years toward the more liberal Kennedy era,

ST was a study of a futuristic military—one wielding a much stronger cultural

influence than the armies found on contemporary Earth. At the same time,

Starship Troopers was a deeply personal work, whose quasi-reactionary poli-

tics continue to fan intellectual debate.

PREPRODUCTION

ST's author, Robert Anson Heinlein, was just as outspoken *as Starship Troopers* itself. Born July 7, 1907, in Butler, Missouri, Heinlein was a voracious reader and ardent admirer of the U.S. Navy. He combined both passions by eventually entering the U.S. Naval Academy in Annapolis, Maryland, in 1925. After graduating and receiving a military commission in 1929, Heinlein served aboard the USS *Lexington* and the destroyer *Roper* before contracting tuberculosis. He was eventually cured of this disease, and retired from active military service in 1934.

For the next thirteen years, Heinlein studied engineering, physics, and mathematics, while simultaneously holding down such odd jobs as silver mining and real estate. He finally tried his hand at writing. Heinlein's reason? To help pay off the mortgage on a house he'd purchased with his first wife.

The sale of Heinlein's first story ("Lifeline," to the prestigious "hard" SF magazine *Astounding Science Fiction*) occured in 1939. He then produced nearly fifty years' worth of extraordinary fiction. And the stylistic elements Heinlein exhibited in his work—strongly American characterizations, fascinating extrapolations on contemporary technology, rock-solid storytelling—were not limited to his many subsequent short stories. Books like *The Puppet Masters* (1951, concerning the attempted takeover of humanity by parasitic aliens from Jupiter's moon Titan) and 1956's *Double Star* (a Hugo Award-winning outer space novel about an actor impersonating a politician of the future) announced the arrival of a first-rate novelist as well.

Heinlein's literary reputation was then cemented with his 1961 crossover hit, *Stranger in a Strange Land.* This wildly successful novel featuring Valentine Michael Smith—a human orphan raised by Martians, who returns to Earth and becomes a New Messiah—landed Heinlein on mainstream best-seller lists.

The author also conquered other markets. In 1950 Heinlien cowrote director George Pal's Academy Award–winning motion picture *Destination Moon.* The year 1950 also saw the premiere of *Tom Corbett, Space Cadet,* a popular children's television show, loosely based on Heinlein's 1948 novel, *Space Cadet.* And 1994 saw Hollywood return to Heinlein's material with a big screen adaptation of *Puppet Masters.*

By the time of his death in 1988, Heinlein had received a "Grand Master" Nebula Award from the Science Fiction Writers' Association and was one of the best-known SF "names" on the planet. Indeed, given the fact that he had such a profound influence on science fiction as we know it, it's not much of a stretch to think of Robert A. Heinlein as the ultimate SF writer.

The Novel

Part of Heinlein's popularity lay in his willingness to strike off in new directions. For instance, his 1948 *Rocket Ship Galileo* (a fanciful tale involving "space soldiers" battling evil Nazis on the moon) became the first of Heinlein's "juvenile novels," books specifically written for the 1950's audience of young, male science fiction addicts. *Galileo* was so popular, in fact, that it spawned a whole series of similarly minded "juveniles" like *Red Planet* (1949), *The Rolling Stones* (1952), *The Star Beast* (1954), and more.

Then came 1959, and *Starship Troopers.*

ST won Heinlein a Hugo Award for Best Novel in 1960. This must have helped salve the author's irritation over the fact that *ST* had originally been rejected by Scribners, Heinlein's longtime publisher, after vague complaints about *Starship Troopers'* "content"—an action which saw the author angrily breaking off all further dealings with Scribner's, to place the book with the Putnam publishing company instead. But Scribner's reaction over *ST* was not to be the last. As Russell F. Letson writes in *The New Encyclopedia of Science Fiction,* "Starship Troopers marked the beginning of a negative shift in the public opinion of Heinlein, especially among liberal critics and readers. . . . Since *Starship Troopers,* Heinlein has been variously characterized as a conservative, a militarist, a libertarian, a solipsist, and even a fascist."

What caused this agitation? A superficial recounting of *Starship Troopers'* story line gives little indication of its power to provoke.

ST begins on a future Earth ruled by an effective worldwide government; daily life is characterized by social harmony and personal responsibility. But this planetwide peace is abruptly disrupted by an extraterrestrial menace—intelligent alien insects called "The Bugs" —who in a surprise attack drop a meteor on the city of Buenos Aires and obliterate it. The result is interstellar war.

ST's remaining story is then observed through the eyes of its young protagonist, Johnny Rico. We watch Rico graduate from high school, join up with the armed forces (the "Mobile Infantry"), and go through basic training at a futuristic Boot Camp, before becoming a planet-hopping Bug-killer.

Two pages from the ST script display how Paul Verhoeven would often jot down notes and drawings on his copy of the screenplay.

Starship Troopers' plot, therefore, was relatively straightforward. Yet its sociopolitical stance was not.

Through the character of Johnny Rico, Heinlein espouses certain ethical and moral issues which have been variously described as reactionary, libertarian, or right-wing. Moreover, *ST*'s planetwide values of discipline, personal responsibility, and sacrifice of the individual for the good of the group—characteristics heartily endorsed by the futuristic, militarist culture under which Rico lives—have resulted in "a society that works," a not-so-subtle slam against the more "liberal" attitudes of the twentieth century (which, at least in Heinlein's view, resulted in a society that didn't work). Additionally, what little crime is left on *Starship Troopers'* Earth is dealt with swiftly and ruthlessly—sometimes by public floggings or hangings.

ST's moral outlook can be summed up by a moment when Johnny Rico, still in high school, listens to a classroom lecture on "History and Moral Responsibility." Its message? That the "permissive" social programs of the late twentieth century resulted in a total breakdown of democracy.

It's easy to see why *Starship Troopers'* glorification of the military caused such an uproar upon its initial release. Heinlein, however, felt that the book's many critics had missed his novel's point. This was made clear in a 1972 *Oui* interview ("Conversation with Robert Heinlein") during which the author stated that:

"[*Starship Troopers* has a] basic theme: that a man, to be truly human, must be unhesitatingly willing at all times to lay down his life for his fellow man. [This theme is] based on the twin concepts of love and duty—and how they are related to the survival of our race."

Regardless of how one interprets Heinlein's voice, however, it's clear that *Starship Troopers* was indeed a novel tract. And perhaps it was exactly this "soapbox" quality which kept the book from being adapted as a motion picture for nearly four decades.

Enter Jon Davison

Eventually, however, *Starship Troopers* did attract the attention of producer Jon Davison. Born in 1949 in Philadelphia, Davison explains that, "My interest in *ST* is a natural one, since I've always had a fascination with science fiction. For instance, as a child I devoured classic SF films like *Them!* and *Forbidden Planet.* Later, during my early high

Giacomo Ghiazzi's storyboards showing the death of Sergeant Gillespie (Curnal Aulisio) at the claws of an alien Hopper Bug.

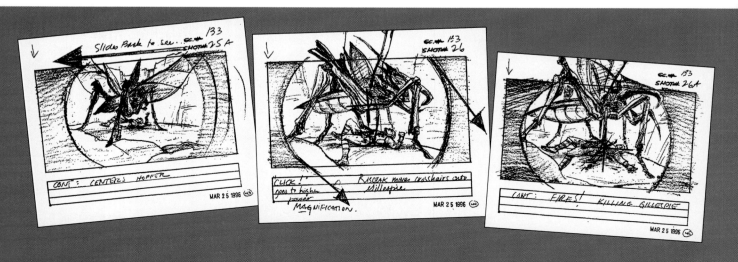

school days, I edited and published a science fiction fanzine, *Cinema X.* So these types of activities exposed me to a wide range of science fiction books, and to the always interesting world of SF fandom."

Davison had broken into the film industry in 1972, by helping rewrite director Jonathan Kaplan's *Night Call Nurses,* the third in a series of soft-core exploitation films generated by legendary low-budget producer Roger Corman. After next producing a number of his own low-budget films (such as 1976's *Hollywood Boulevard,* director Joe "*Gremlins*" Dante's first feature credit), Davison hit the mainstream as the producer of the box-office hit *Airplane!* in 1980.

Yet it was another Davison success—1987's *RoboCop,* the story of a murdered Detroit policeman resurrected as a crime-fighting cyborg—that had a more direct influence on the making of *Starship Troopers.* For *RoboCop* first united Davison with director Paul Verhoeven, screenwriter Edward Neumeier, and special effects ace Phil Tippett—the same creative triumvirate later attached to *ST* itself.

As Davison recalls, "Long before I ever met Paul Verhoeven I'd admired his films. Then, after we worked together on *RoboCop,* I came to respect Paul as well. He's an incredibly talented, experienced, and well-prepared filmmaker. I'd also enjoyed Ed Neumeier; it was a lot of fun working with him, too. But *Starship Troopers* really happened because of my desire to get something new off the ground with the third point of the *RoboCop* triangle, Phil Tippett."

A much-respected special effects artist who has worked with Steven Spielberg and George Lucas (among others), Tippett had been responsible for using an F/X process called stop-motion animation to bring *RoboCop*'s murderous "Enforcement Droid" ED-209 to life. He had also worked with Davison on the latter's 1990 production of *RoboCop 2,* and on the 1978 Davison-produced *Piranha.*

"The reason I keep working with Phil is because I really esteem his work," Davison points out. "And I'm always trying to find things we can do together. For example, in 1987, Phil and I developed this idea for a very unique dinosaur movie, one that was in development before *Jurassic Park,* which Paul Verhoeven had agreed to direct for Disney. But though Disney loved the script, Verhoeven and I could not agree with that studio regarding the manner in which Disney wanted to do the special effects. So Paul, Phil, and I left that project. However, I then kept working on yet another idea, one I thought would make an excellent forum to show off Phil Tippett's work."

This "other idea" had been brought to Davison's attention by Edward Neumeier—*ST*'s eventual screenwriter.

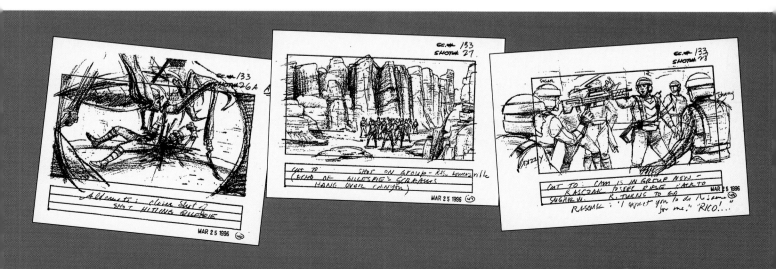

The Screenwriter

Ed Neumeier was born in 1957 in Vienna, and grew up in the middle-class suburbs of San Francisco. "I realized early on that I'd probably wind up as a writer, which had always been one of my passions," Neumeier recalls. "I also loved film. Two of the earliest pictures to influence me were *Lawrence of Arabia* and *Help!,* with the Beatles—which would make an interesting double bill, come to think of it."

Following his bliss, Neumeier attended UCLA Film School. He later worked in Hollywood as both a script reader (a studio employee who passes judgment on whether or not a specific written property is worth cultivating) and a development executive at Universal Pictures. "But I was unhappy in the role of a 'suit,' as studio executives are commonly referred to," Neumeier continues. "So I began scripting a story entitled *RoboCop,* with my then writing partner Michael Miner."

Soon after *RoboCop*'s success, Neumeier and Miner wrote the opening segment for a Canadian-based *RoboCop* television series. "And after the two *Robos,*" Neumeier says, "I worked on a bunch of things with Michael, none of which panned out. In retrospect, I think I was trying too hard to manage the politics of a writing partnership while chasing all the deals which are offered after you've written a hit movie. What I should have done was sit down and do something I wanted to do."

Acting on those instincts, Neumeier severed his ties with Miner to strike out on his own. "And eventually, I came up with an idea I felt was a pretty sturdy one," the writer concludes.

An idea which Neumeier now carried to his old *RoboCop* producer, Jon Davison.

Bug Hunt at *Outpost 7*

"Around December of '91," recalls Jon Davison, "Ed came to visit me at the Warner Brothers studio in Burbank, where TriStar Pictures, with whom I had a development deal, was then headquartered. At that time I was also sharing an office on the Warners lot with a marvelous woman named Frances Dole, with whom I was trying to develop various projects. That's why she gets a coproducer credit on *Starship Troopers,* even though we later amicably parted company; Frances was there at the beginning.

"Anyway, Ed and I were walking across a parking lot at Warners one afternoon when he suddenly said, 'You know, I've got this idea. It's an outer space movie about killing giant insects.'"

Neumeier then related the skeleton of a plot concerning a lonely soldier posted on a planet harboring huge alien insects. Davison was intrigued by the concept. The writer's idea "not only sounded commercial, but seemed like an excellent forum to show off the work of Phil Tippett," Davison recalls.

"I also told Jon," Neumeier continues, "that I wanted to do a war movie. One that started with a futuristic battle, flashed back to a high school teenage romance, then proceeded from there. And I really wanted this picture to feature a vintage, xenophobic enemy, which in this case would be giant killer insects. 'You mean, something like *Starship Troopers*?' Jon asked me. 'Yeah,' I said. That's when I discovered we'd both read *Starship Troopers* as kids."

Davison picks up the thread. "I first read Heinlein's book in junior high school, after it had been given to me by John Woods, who was my 'science fiction friend' from that period. I remember thinking *then* that it would make a fantastic movie. Many years later, though, when the novel came up in my conversation with Ed, he and I were sure that at least four thousand other people had probably already optioned the rights to Heinlein's book. We were so sure that we didn't have a chance of getting it, in fact, that I encouraged Ed to try and work up something original. I said, 'Okay, let's do a little treatment and see how your idea fleshes out.'

"Ed then went away for a long period and did that treatment," Davison says. "I think it ended up being called *Outpost 7*."

Jump-cut to the fall of 1992. By now, Davison and Dole had relocated their office to the Culver City-based Sony Pictures Studio, home of both Columbia and TriStar Pictures. It was here that Neumeier brought the producer the completed *Outpost 7* treatment.

Davison was more than satisfied with Neumeier's effort. In fact, the producer was so taken with one *Outpost* sequence—a kinetic battle featuring overgrown insects—that Davison began referring to Neumeier's effort as *Bug Hunt*. Whatever its official title, the producer now set up a meeting with TriStar Pictures executive Chris Lee, in order to propose Neumeier's new project.

"We met with Chris," Davison continues, "pitched him verbally and he turned us down."

Yet this refusal did not discourage the pair. Davison knew that a "no" at this stage of the game was not always written in stone, "So Ed and I went right back to my office to discuss ways to make Chris Lee change his mind," the producer continues. "One of the things that came up—again—was Heinlein's book. Even though I was sure that they had probably already been snapped up, Ed was just as strong in his opinion that we should look into the novel's rights situation. Because *Starship Troopers* had giant bugs in it. And we *wanted* those bugs.

On location in Hell's Half-Acre, producer Alan Marshall scans the horizon for marauding studio executives.

"So, not really expecting anything, we inquired about optioning Heinlein's novel. Lo and behold, we discovered it was still available! Whereupon Ed and I immediately went back to Chris Lee and said, 'We want to make Robert Heinlein's *Starship Troopers*!'"

Reaction this time was more positive; it also came from more than one source. Davison's *Troopers* proposal had found another, more influential supporter, in TriStar's then head of production, Mike Medavoy, who had performed a similar function at Orion Pictures when Davison and Neumeier had made *RoboCop* there. Perhaps sensing that a reunion of the original *Robo* team could result in lightning striking twice, Medavoy let it be known that he too was an enthusiastic backer of a possible *Starship Troopers* film.

"Suddenly," as Jon Davison recounts, "TriStar became interested. We got approval from the studio to go ahead and develop this movie, TriStar took out an option on Heinlein's novel, and Ed was hired to begin writing a script."

Tippett Studio

In order to keep studio interest alive in his embryonic project, however, Davison felt it imperative to acquire even more resources. Therefore, not long after Neumeier had retired to his Eagle Rock, California-based office to begin working on the first round of *ST*-oriented screenwriting, Davison concentrated on adding another important element to the nascent *Starship Troopers* mix—the film's giant Big Bugs.

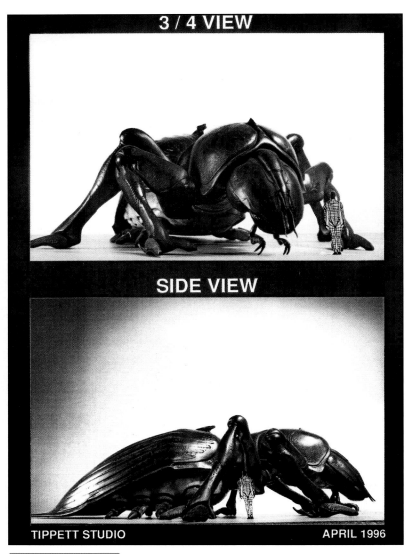

3 / 4 VIEW

SIDE VIEW

TIPPETT STUDIO   **APRIL 1996**

This early Tanker Bug design shows the relative scale of humans to ST's acid-spewing insect.

"At first Ed did a number of *ST* story treatments," the producer explains. "Then, once we thought we had a story nailed, or at least the shape of a story nailed, we approached Phil Tippett with those treatments, in order to show him our thoughts about visualizing the Bugs. Of course, Phil already knew about our involvement with *Starship Troopers*. What we didn't know was how he'd react to our ideas."

"Phil Tippett was in on this project very early on," adds Neumeier. "In fact, the first outline I ever wrote started with a scene of Federation scientists torturing a Bug pilot. That was then sent off to Tippett, who said something like, 'Well, this is cool. But it seems kind of long . . . and what's that Bug pilot going to look like?' So Phil was already turning over story problems and creature designs in his head."

Long years in the special effects field had taught Tippett the value of such habits. He'd first gained widespread attention in 1977 for animating the "living chess pieces" seen in *Star Wars.* After moving on to bigger projects—*The Empire Strikes Back* (1980), *Dragonslayer* (1981), *Dragonheart* (1996)—Tippett gained an industrywide reputation as a skilled F/X craftsman with a special affinity for stop-motion animation. This laborious special effects process involves manually manipulating meticulously detailed puppets in tiny, incremental movements on miniature soundstages, after which figures are photographed frame by frame while live-action footage is projected on small screens behind them.

Tippett's experience in this technique resulted in two Academy Awards for special effects, one for his work on *Return of the Jedi* (1983), the other for *Jurassic Park* (1993). It was partially because of *Jurassic Park* that Tippett agreed to take on what would ultimately prove to be an enormous number of *Starship Troopers'* "Bug shots."

"Prior to *Jurassic*," the personable, sandy-haired F/X master clarifies, "I and the employees in my company, Tippett Studio, produced stop-motion through mostly traditional methods—that is, moving three-dimensional puppets by hand. But the dinosaurs for *Jurassic* were *not* created traditionally. Instead, a special piece of equipment was developed for that picture called the Digital Input Device. The basic principle behind it is fairly simple: the DID electronically links a small metal armature, or skeleton, of whatever creature you're trying to animate straight to a desktop computer. So if a stop-motion animator moves this armature by hand, those movements directly translate to a wire-frame model of that armature in the computer. That's partially how the dinosaurs of *Jurassic Park* were brought to life.

"As pleased as we were with the CG [computer-generated] dinosaur shots we did for *Jurassic,* though," Tippett continues, "I always felt there was room for improvement. The software, the hardware, the time it took to render out images—all that needed refinement. So when Jon Davison approached me about doing *Starship Troopers,* I realized that not only could Tippett Studio use the DID to help create those Bugs, we could also take enormous steps forward in other CG techniques we'd begun using on *Jurassic Park.*"

"Thank God Phil decided to do *Starship*," adds Davison. "Without him, we wouldn't have had a movie!"

The Director

During Phil Tippett's start-up period, *Starship Troopers'* screenwriter had spent "a good three or four months working on a solid outline to the script I intended to write. And by early 1993," Neumeier continues, "I'd finished that outline. Not long after, I gathered it up and met with the only director Jon and I had ever thought was right for this picture."

That director was Paul Verhoeven, a key Hollywood player whose string of past hits certainly made him *ST*'s most bankable element. But why—other than the fact that Neumeier and Davison had worked with the Dutch-born director on *RoboCop*—were the *ST* developers so certain that Verhoeven was the best candidate for *Starship Troopers*?

"Because I think Paul basically *likes* these kind of films," said Davison. "He's also a film

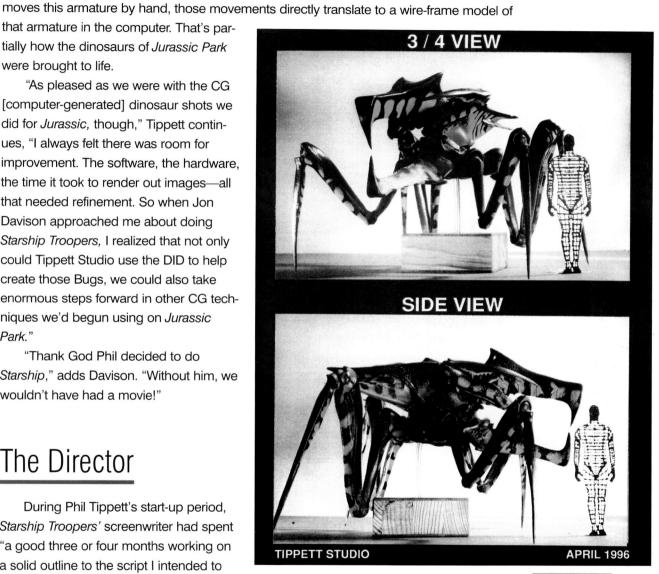

*Tippett Studio's
Warrior Bug maquette.*

buff. Take the Ray Harryhausen classics—*Seventh Voyage of Sinbad, Mysterious Island;* all those motion pictures in which Harryhausen created these amazing creatures from fantasy and mythology—those are a part of Paul's filmic vocabulary. Plus, I was sure he'd be intrigued by a large-scale science fiction action picture that had a serious political undertone to it."

Intelligent, fiercely energetic, quick-witted and occasionally sharp-tongued, Paul Verhoeven was born in Amsterdam in 1938 to a middle-class family. Verhoeven's memories of his home life remain "comfortable." But the future film director also grew up in The Hague, the German center for occupied Holland, during World War II. And his family lived very close—"only a mile or two"—to the launching site of the Dutch-based German V1 and V2 rockets. "Which meant that the Americans were constantly trying to bomb those facilities," Verhoeven recalls. "But I was just a young boy with no scale of reference. These massive explosions were just everyday life to me, the best and most impressive special effects."

It is often said that "the child is father to the man." Was it his early exposure to the horrors of warfare, then, which were responsible for the later, intensely realized scenes of death and violence Verhoeven mounted for such graphic motion pictures as *RoboCop, Total Recall,* and *Basic Instinct*?

"These WWII childhood experiences, to a certain extent, I'm sure, have resulted in the type of artist I am," the accented and articulate Dutch director says. "For example, a lot of war was constantly going on around me. All those childhood images and experiences are still locked up in me, which is probably why I always carry around these feelings of tension and extremity—which anyway are for me, somehow, the natural state of a human being. A life on the edge, you could say."

Verhoeven's "life-on-the-edge" approach was put to good use during his early career as a director in Holland. Such Dutch motion pictures as *Turkish Delight, Spetters* and *The 4th Man* made him the Netherlands' most commercially successful fimmaker. Interestingly, the director's most personal project during this period (and one which moviegoers looking for celluloid clues to Verhoeven's true personality are advised to study) was also one of his most popular—*Soldier of Orange* (1977). A multilayered story concerning a group of Dutch college students caught up in the Nazi invasion of Holland, *Soldier* can also be seen as a "dry run" for the equally combat-oriented *Starship Troopers.*

Paul Verhoeven eventually left Holland for America and American-style filmmaking. This resulted in a trio of box-office successes: the darkly satirical *RoboCop,* the 1990 science fiction adventure *Total Recall,* and the sexually charged *Basic Instinct* (1992). Yet ironically, when he was approached to do *Starship Troopers,* Verhoeven was experiencing one of those periodic downswings which seem to inevitably afflict the careers of even the most successful filmmakers. Two expensive, prestige-laden projects slated for Verhoeven direction during this period—Columbia's *Mistress of the Seas,* a female pirate adventure, and Carolco Pictures' *The Crusade,* intended to star Arnold Schwarzenegger—never reached fruition. Moreover, Verhoeven had also embarked on the project that would ultimately earn him the worst reviews of his career—the soon-to-be-notorious Las Vegas melodrama *Showgirls* (1995).

Of course, at this point Verhoeven had no way of knowing that *Showgirls* would fail. And as he was already committed to begin shooting this project, Verhoeven "told Ed

Neumeier and Jon Davison that I could not make *Starship Troopers* until I finished this other picture. I wasn't trying to put them off, though," Verhoeven says. "I really wanted to make this movie from Robert Heinlein's book. But not until after *Showgirls.*

"Still, there were really a number of reasons I decided to do *Starship,*" the director continues. "For one, I like science fiction movies. I mean, the *Star Wars* series is delightful, you know? I really liked the first and the second of those films, and have an enormous respect for what George Lucas achieved there—that mixture of 'hard' science fiction and fantasy, the audacity to do that. *Star Wars* put science fiction in a completely new category.

"But the main reason I decided to do *Starship Troopers* was Phil Tippett. I had worked with Phil on *RoboCop,* and felt that that was really interesting; the effects Phil did for that picture were fascinating. So I very much wanted to work with Phil again. This is why, when Jon Davison and Ed Neumeier came to me with *Starship Troopers,* I thought, 'Okay, perhaps we can try again with Phil. Let's see what can be done on a motion picture with, essentially, two different directors—with Phil as the director of the creatures, and I as the director of the people.'"

An ST Art Department worker examines a miniature reference model of the Camp Currie obstacle course.

Verhoeven's agreement, however, came with a codicil: Once the director began *Starship Troopers,* his *Showgirls* producer, Alan Marshall (also producer of *Basic Instinct*), would likewise become part of the *ST* team—meaning that should the film ever go into production, it would have two separate-but-equal producers.

Happily, Jon Davison had no problem with this arrangement. "Alan is a terrific producer," Davison says. "I welcomed his expertise."

The First-Draft Script

Edward Neumeier finished a first-draft *ST* screenplay on July 8, 1993.

But where did Neumeier's script take Heinlein's story? After all, the source material had been generating controversy since its original appearance in 1959.

"One of our first concerns was the tone of Heinlein's book," Davison admits. "In fact, I used to be the secretary of the Philadelphia Science Fiction Society in my early high school days, and also used to subscribe to lots of fanzines. And I can still remember, even years after its initial publication, the storm of controversy surrounding, quote, 'Robert Heinlein's fascist novel *Starship Troopers*,' unquote.

"So that was definitely a primary concern—how were we going to deal with this? Our answer was, by being faithful to our source. Ed and I agreed early on that there was no point in doing Robert Heinlein's *Starship Troopers* and then changing his viewpoint."

"What I really liked about the idea of this movie was that it allowed me to write about fascism," Neumeier elaborates. "That's amusing. It was also difficult to do—or to do well. Paul Verhoeven had an enormous influence on that angle of the picture, once he became more actively involved. But right from the start, I had a feeling that today's film audiences would really appreciate Heinlein's ideas. Because the message of the original book was pretty straightforward: Democracy is failing, and we need some strict controls on our culture.

"I retained that outlook in the *ST* scripts. But I also wanted to play with it. To me, the whole spin of the movie is this: You want a world that works? Okay, we'll show you one. And it really *does* work. It happens to be a military dictatorship, but it works. That was the original rhythm I was trying to play with, just to sort of mess with the audience. It'll be interesting to see if it works."

"The other major headache we inherited from Heinlein's novel was structural," continues Davison. "Heinlein's *Starship Troopers* has a strong first and third act. But most of the middle portion of the novel, the part where Johnny Rico is in boot camp, is basically a tract; Heinlein is preaching to his readership there. Well, that's fine for a book, but not necessarily the sort of thing that a major studio is going to invest millions of dollars in.

ST production designer Allan Cameron.

"On the other hand, Ed and I felt that there was still enough good stuff in Heinlein's book to use as a springboard. Others obviously have felt the same way, since this novel has been unofficially used for other movies. Certainly *Aliens* was heavily influenced by *Starship Troopers,* as was that 1995 TV show *Space: Above and Beyond.*

"Up until we tried, though, I honestly think no one else approached Heinlein's novel with the thought of doing a faithful adaptation. But Ed pulled that off. He did a fantastic job of preserving Heinlein's essential elements—the high school opening, boot camp, the battle scenes, the insects, the philosophizing—and then made it work on its own terms, as a screenplay."

Besides retaining the original novel's controversial sociopolitics, Neumeier's first-draft script also attempted to work around the book's chat-filled central section. "I did that by elaborating upon the characters and ideas Heinlein had already set up in *Starship Troopers'* opening and closing," explains the screenwriter. "The high school scenes, for example; I was thinking a lot about my own high school experiences there, which at some level involved chasing girls who weren't interested in you. But what I basically tried to do was logically expand upon the narrative already found in Heinlein's novel. Hopefully, readers familiar with the book will watch the film and say, 'Yeah. At least this *could* happen.'"

Although numerous aspects of *Starship*-the-motion-picture would ultimately depart from its source material, Neumeier points out that his first-draft script actually *mirrored* Heinlein's novel. "In fact, I initially tried to stay fairly faithful to the book. For instance, a lot of Heinlein's original material—this other alien race called the Skinnies; the Bounce, which was a sort of jet-assisted way ground troops could shoot up into the air; the weapons-laden Power Armor which the troopers wore—all of that was in my first draft. I knew a lot of this would change if we ever went into production, though," Neumeier concludes with a shrug. "Screenplays always do."

Politics

"At this point we had a full script, and one of the first things we did with that," picks up Jon Davison, "was to send a copy to Virginia Heinlein, Robert's widow. We wanted to get her reaction on our work. From what I later heard from her agent, Virginia read the script and did not seem unhappy. In fact, Heinlein's widow actually seemed rather pleased by it other than to say, 'Well, I see they've changed some things. But I guess that's what Hollywood does.'"

Another result of Neumeier's first draft was that Davison could now begin preparing a thorough *ST* budget breakdown to submit for TriStar's approval. Months later, however—after that breakdown had been duly completed by the *ST* production company, which eventually would take on the business name Big Bug Pictures in order to generate this one project—TriStar looked at the proposed costs and balked. Why? Because the initial estimate totaled approximately $90 million. TriStar insisted this figure be reduced, although an amount of $100 million would later be quoted many times in the popular press as *ST*'s overall budget.

"This happens all the time in Hollywood," Davison explains. "In order to get a picture made, you first turn in the budget that you think is realistic. Then the studio always says that you have to cut back a little. So you turn that revised estimate in and they say, 'You have to cut back a little bit more.' You do that and they say, 'Just one more set of cuts.' So you do *that* last set of cuts and they say 'Okay.' Of course, the first number you turned in was always the right number.

"But in *Starship Troopers'* case, the studio didn't seem to think so—maybe because at the time, there was the matter of this little picture called *Waterworld*. The studio mentioned *Waterworld* at almost every *ST* meeting I attended; the reason, of course, was that *Waterworld* had supposedly cost around two hundred million, been a disappointing box-office performer, and been branded as an example of Hollywood excess. It also was one of the things which killed an entire management regime at Universal Pictures that had been in place for many years. At the same time, a managerial shake-up was also going on at Sony Pictures, one that eventually resulted in Mike Medavoy, our first and biggest booster, leaving TriStar. So I understood that our own studio execs were worrying about their jobs.

"On the other hand," Davison emphasizes, "and I said this more than once, *Starship Troopers* wasn't going to be another *Waterworld*. In my own humble opinion, our movie was going to be a lot more economically manageable."

Birth of the Bugs

Big Bug Pictures now began focusing on the giant insects after which it had been named. First it was agreed that everything to do with the film's Bugs would be the sole responsibility of Tippett Studio. This agreement, in turn, dictated the next logical step in the Bug process: Since Phil Tippett had by now decided *how* to animate these creatures (via the Digital Input Device and other, more conventional computer animation methods), what were Heinlein's Bugs going to *look* like? And who would actually design them?

Jon Davison supplies the answers:

"One of the most important employees at Tippett Studio, besides Phil, is a guy named Craig Hayes. He's an exceptionally talented industrial artist, a wonderful mechanical engineer, and a great props and electronics-design expert. Craig first collaborated with Phil in 1985, on the look and construction of *RoboCop*'s full-scale ED-209. I'd thought that was terrific. So when Phil suggested Craig be the one to start designing *Starship Troopers'* Bugs with him, I said, 'Sure!'"

Actually, the final "look" of *ST*'s Bugs was something of a collaborative process between Hayes, Tippett, Davison, and Neumeier—"and Paul Verhoeven," Phil Tippett points out. "*Especially* Paul. But really, the bottom line was this—it was Craig Hayes who sat down with pencil and paper and designed our insects."

Before those initial drawings could be created, however, certain fundamental concepts had to be locked into place, as Ed Neumeier explains:

"One of the earliest *ST* things Paul Verhoeven and I talked about were the Bugs. Paul asked me, 'What do they look like?' And I said, 'Well, they're only vaguely described in the book. However, the Bugs seem to be able to shoot guns and behave in an anthropomorphic way, even though Heinlein says they look like spiders.' And as Paul and I kept talking, it became clear that our discussion was leading along a path that George Lucas had already blazed—designing anthropomorphic aliens portrayed by actors in costumes. But Verhoeven quickly stopped that. He told me, 'No, I'm not ready for this: I can't see a Bug holding a gun.' Put that way, I immediately knew what Paul meant. Verhoeven didn't want to see some sort of man-in-a-suit with a funny crab claw, or an upright, six-foot-tall ant with its head in a space helmet. Those had already been done to death. So what we eventually came up with," Neumeier concludes, "was the idea that we should do the Bugs *as* bugs—as giant insects."

Taking their cue from Verhoeven's concept, Hayes and Tippett now began a furious period of Bug design. As a result, the film's various insects (a total of six different types) were conceived well in advance of *Starship Troopers'* preproduction period. "Most of the Bug designs were pretty much finalized by the end of 1993," elaborates Jon Davison.

"During that year, Phil Tippett and Craig Hayes would come down from Phil's effects facility up in San Francisco with sketches—the look of the Bugs was first worked out on paper—and then Paul and Ed and I would hunker down and make comments. Craig, though, did the actual Bug designs themselves. With, of course, input from Phil, who was Craig's supervisor and in overall charge of every Bug sequence you see in the picture."

"Craig Hayes can speak about this in a much more articulate manner than I," Tippett picks up, "but at this point we weren't really giving the pantomime, or movements, of the Bugs too much thought. Craig instead went for overall visual impressions. The performance angles of these insects—the considerably more complicated process of trying to figure out what, for these creatures, would be a realistic gait, or coming up with actions they could do—came much later. Basically, Craig's first task on *Starship Troopers* was to come up with something the director wanted.

"You see, Paul Verhoeven has a particular aesthetic that is considerably more hard-edged than, say, a Lucas or a Spielberg, who tend to be softer, fuzzier, and a little bit cuter. Paul is more visceral. So Craig definitely took Verhoeven's outlook into consideration. That meant the Bugs of *Starship Troopers* were going to have to be fast, mean, and ferocious. But then there was this question: 'How are we actually going to *do* these Bugs?' I mean, obviously we were going to use computer graphics methods to produce the insects themselves. But the sheer volume and complexity of *ST*'s CG Bugs was going to surpass anything Tippett Studio had ever attempted.

"To give you some idea of our workload, we eventually worked out that we'd have to provide about two hundred CG Bug shots for *ST*—*Jurassic Park* had less than fifty! So a great deal of the look of the Bugs was worked out and designed with the thought of us actually being able to produce them."

As Craig Hayes explains, designing the giant Bugs of *Starship Troopers* also demanded "drama and believability. Those were the two rules all the Bug designs had to satisfy. It only made sense to take that route," Hayes continues, "because Phil and Paul have a much stronger background in filmmaking and theatrical dramatics than I do. So at first we'd begin by talking about the Bugs in terms of their *dramatic* background. What did these insect characters need to do? What kind of presence should they have? What was their character motivation? Those basic questions Paul and Phil saw as very important. From there, I'd work up some drawings that tried to visualize the answers to those questions."

However, Hayes'

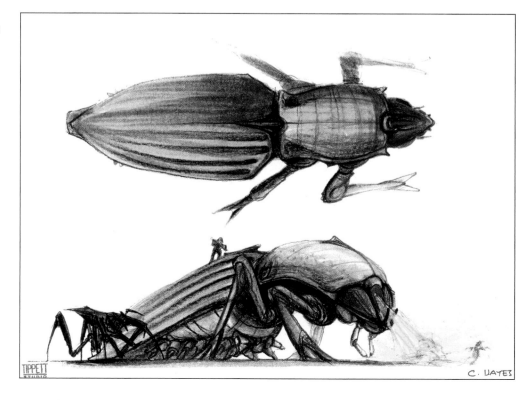

visual "answers" to the look of *ST*'s Bugs did not stop with their appearance. As the designer reveals, great care and consideration was also given to include a believable social framework for each *Starship Troopers* insect.

"Early on, we decided the *ST* Bugs would mimic the hierarchal structure real insects follow in nature: workers, drones, queens," Hayes points out. "And since this was going to be a combat movie, it seemed only logical to conclude that a Bug society would also incorporate some sort of insect infantry—a nonhuman analog to the soldiers on our side. From that line of thought came a class of Bugs we called the Warriors, who are the alien foot soldiers, maybe even the small tanks, of the Bug army.

"At the same time, we wanted to emphasize believability—though we also knew that the basic idea of this movie was pretty fantastic. So we then agreed that the best way to get an audience to accept our giant insects was to make most of them as familiar and realistic as possible. That's one reason we chose to make the Warrior Bugs hard-shelled ground crawlers; they look something like crickets or roaches or staghorn beetles, with a couple of praying mantis–type attack claws. Plus a beak or horn that could really gouge and damage you. We did that because the Warriors had to be able to chase somebody down and cause them harm.

"Anyway," Hayes concludes, "using logic and drama as our guidelines, the Bug designs from that point on became a fairly progressive process."

The Bug Test

By now it was early 1994. Yet despite the fact that Big Bug Pictures had packaged a finished script, a committed director, an Oscar-winning special effects supervisor, and giant insect designs for its proposed motion picture, TriStar still had not given *Starship Troopers* the green light to move it out of development and into pre-production. Frustrated by these delays, Verhoeven and his colleagues began conferring on other methods to move *Starship Troopers* forward more quickly.

"At this juncture we agreed the best way to energize this thing was to shoot some test footage," Jon Davison says, "sort of like a short, in-house promo film. If we came up with something exciting, we felt that might convince TriStar to finance our picture."

Work on this promotional film—ultimately running under two minutes in length, and later known as the "Bug Test"—began with story conferences. Since all involved agreed that the real stars of *Starship Troopers* were its giant insects (regardless of which human actors were ultimately signed for the project), it was also

Final Craig Hayes designs for the Chariot Bugs.

decided that the most effective Bug Test would be one that dynamically showcased *ST*'s extraterrestrial arachnids.

Therefore, a short, kinetic sequence showing two ferocious Warrior Bugs chasing and killing a futuristic foot soldier was devised. "Yet while all this Bug Test preparation was going on, Paul Verhoeven was still involved with *Showgirls,*" Davison recalls. "However, Paul had made it clear that he'd find time to actually direct this test footage himself, once we locked in the details.

"So the Bug Test now went through several storyboard incarnations. Then Phil Tippett put his input into those boards, with the result that our concept narrowed down quite closely to what we ultimately shot. We nailed it down so closely, in fact, that the Warrior Bug design—which of course the Bug Test prominently features—really hasn't changed much since then. Their coloration is somewhat different, and the edges and joints of their bodies are somewhat different. But the basic Warrior was locked in by that test—which determined, by the way, the overall *size* of a Warrior Bug, too. In its normal standing position, a Warrior is between six and eight feet tall, and fourteen feet long.

"In any event," concludes Davison, "Paul Verhoeven then signed off on these concepts. Next we got TriStar Pictures to underwrite the actual production costs for the Bug Test—which were around two hundred twenty-five thousand dollars—and not long after, Paul went out and directed it."

The Bug Test was shot on location at Vasquez Rocks, California, just outside Los Angeles, on July 21, 1994. A one-day shoot, the test was filmed by John Hora (frequent cinematographer for director Joe Dante). Crew size was minimal, similar to those employed on small-scale television commercials—approximately twenty-five to thirty people. Starring in the Bug Test—as the hapless trooper who is chased by two Warriors, manages to shoot one to pieces, and then is brought down by its arachnid companion—was Mitch Gaylord, former Olympic gymnast. Edward Neumeier also put in a cameo appearance, playing a dead trooper surrounded by other eviscerated corpses (dummies manufactured by the KNB F/X group). Most of the footage shot that day was of a variety called a "live-action plate"—"clean" frames of film showing only the human actors, props, and surrounding scenery, onto which the computer-generated Warriors would later be digitally added by Tippett Studio.

Yet even then, the Bug Test would not be fully complete.

Not until the day it was screened for those all-important TriStar executives capable of underwriting *Starship Troopers'* next stage of cinematic evolution.

Amalgamated Dynamics Inc.'s conceptual art for the "Arkellian Sand Beetle" dissected during ST's high school scenes. This was the only "Bug" in Starship Troopers *not designed by Tippett Studio.*

Rewrites

Although shooting the Bug Test had only required a single day, finishing postproduction work for this "demo" version of *Starship Troopers* took months. Final visuals and CG effects (including an opening sequence of Paul Verhoeven introducing the Bug Test, shot while the director was filming *Showgirls* in Las Vegas, and a closing *ST* title graphic provided by Peter Kuran, of Visual Concepts Engineering) were not completely finished and/or inserted into the Vasquez Rocks footage until September 1994. A punchy, arresting sound track (mixed by Steve Flick) was then completed the following month.

Finally, by early October, Big Bug's crucial "visual proposal" was ready for viewing by the TriStar studio heads. "I thought Paul Verhoeven and Phil Tippett had done a terrific job with the test; their footage was every bit as exciting and dynamic as I'd hoped. But TriStar's reaction," continues Jon Davison, chuckling, ". . . well, that was somewhat less than expected. The studio execs sort of sat there and tried to comprehend that it wasn't real, I think; they couldn't quite seem to understand that the Bugs had really been done

with a computer. However, they were certainly impressed enough to give us the go-ahead to take the next steps."

Unfortunately, what the studio sanctioned Big Bug Pictures to move forward on proved to be a protracted, hazily defined process of part development, part preproduction. "Which was frustrating," notes Ed Neumeier. "Because after the Bug Test screening, we *seemed* to be green-lit. Enough TriStar money kept coming in to keep working; Sony allowed us to spend as if we were going into preproduction, knowing full well that those costs would later be charged against the production itself. But that's normal studio procedure.

"However, we actually went through some terrible times. Basically, TriStar wouldn't commit. There were endless disagreements over the budget and, with the exceptions of Chris Lee and Mark Canton, the main executive who'd sort of inherited Medavoy's position, I don't think anybody else at TriStar got what this picture was all about."

Whatever the reasons for this corporate dragging of feet, Big Bug now found itself locked into a state of studio-imposed limbo that would linger for another full year.

Still, the core *Starship Troopers* team remained active. Davison's previously mentioned $90 million budget breakdown, for example, was submitted in the spring of 1995. *ST* script rewrites and conceptual art pieces were also ferried between Big Bug Pictures and Carolco, the production company where Verhoeven was based while making *Showgirls*.

"And even though Paul was still tied up with *Showgirls*," says Ed Neumeier, "he remained a good friend of *Starship Troopers*. For instance, the key change in the second-draft *ST* script [finished in January 1994] was all Paul's doing. And it was a brilliant idea. But to appreciate it, you first have to step back and realize three other things.

"First, I'd always wanted to inject a romantic element into *Starship Troopers*. To do that I'd changed Heinlein's plot, so that the Johnny Rico character was chasing after one of his high school classmates, a young woman named Carmen. Now, Carmen appears in the original novel, but not as Johnny's high school love interest. Also in my original script—and in Heinlein's book—there's a guy named Dizzy Flores, who was one of Johnny's high school friends. Finally, there was a character I'd invented for my script who was *not* in the book. This was a girl named Ronnie, the quarterback of the high school football team, who was aggressively pursuing Johnny because she was romantically interested in him.

"Anyway, Paul looked at all this and said, 'Why don't you combine the characters of Ronnie and Dizzy and make Dizzy into a girl?' That was a great idea. Because when Dizzy changed into a girl, it really made other things click. For example, I'd already come up with the idea of a romantic triangle involving Carmen, Johnny, and Zander [a pilot to whom Carmen is attracted during her fleet training], but Paul's gender switch on the Dizzy character prompted a second, opposing romantic triangle—Johnny, Carmen, and Dizzy! So that was one of the really terrific early ideas Paul had."

However, while 1994 produced some forward movement for the nascent *Starship Troopers,* most of the following year was a different story.

Jon Davison recalls, "1995 was essentially eaten up by a lot of cold feet on the studio's part, and by constant lobbying on Big Bug's part to get the picture made. It became very frustrating. TriStar had decided that the only way they were going to make this picture happen was if Sony could find a corporate partner to help them absorb *ST*'s costs. But they couldn't seem to find that partner. Meanwhile, I kept running around and screening the Bug Test for anyone who'd look at it. I must have shown it to everyone on the lot!"

By now, Neumeier had completed a third-draft screenplay and embarked on yet another version. A large suite of rooms located within the lower floor of the Astaire Building on the Sony lot had been given over to Big Bug Pictures to serve as *Starship Troopers'* official production office. And Tippett Studio began actively hiring digital animators, artists, and engineers to begin preparing for *ST*'s immense CG Bug load.

Yet even though the walls of Big Bug's new office were soon festooned with colorful artworks depicting exotically suited space soldiers and deadly Bugs, the mood within the suite was anything but joyful. That most crucial of studio concessions—the all-important green light—still had not been turned on. This factor, plus the noncommittal attitude TriStar seemed to have adopted toward Big Bug's project, suffused the atmosphere within the fledgling *ST* production office with a low-key air of anxiety.

Then in September 1995, Paul Verhoeven and Alan Marshall finished *Showgirls*. And at last, the official beginning of *Starship*'s preproduction period arrived.

Mr. Marshall, I Presume

September of '95 brought another crucial development as well. As Jon Davison relates, "Sony had spent months trying to find a partner to share *Starship Troopers'* production costs. And eventually Disney Studios showed some interest in that partnership. But it wasn't until September, when Paul and Alan Marshall sat down with representatives from both companies, that Disney officially came onboard."

This critical meeting involved Mark Canton and Marc Platt, from Sony Studios, and Joe Roth, head of Disney's motion picture group. Big Bug was represented by Verhoeven, Marshall, Davison, and Tom Hansen, Verhoeven's entertainment attorney. What eventually transpired was a two-way partnership. Sony and Disney would split the costs of making *Starship Troopers* down the middle; in return, Disney would retain all foreign distribution rights. Sony/TriStar garnered domestic American rights, with all revenue going into one pot.

Disney's now-official *ST* involvement pumped new energy into the Big Bug suite. The first sign of this galvanization was the presence of Verhoeven and Marshall, who not only settled into their new *ST* offices that fall, but began adding their considerable expertise to the task of pushing *Starship Troopers* into production.

Alan Marshall had started his show business career as a messenger boy. "In advertising, for British television in the late 1950s," he recalls. "I then went into editing. That was the only thing that interested me. Whenever I could avoid having to run a message, I was in the cutting rooms watching people cut commercials or movies."

A stint editing commercials, feature films, and documentaries followed before Marshall "was asked by an ad agency to produce commercials. I had no idea how to produce a commercial; somehow, I muddled through. I later met Alan Parker, who at that time was one of the most famous advertising copywriters in England. Alan and I then formed the Alan Parker Film Company, to make both commercials and movies. I subsequently was Parker's producer for nearly nineteen years."

This relationship generated such films as *Bugsy Malone, Midnight Express, Fame, Shoot the Moon, Birdy, Pink Floyd: The Wall,* and *Angel Heart.* But by 1989, Marshall had left the Parker Film Company and produced *Jacob's Ladder* for director Adrian Lyne. "I was then offered a position as head of physical production at Carolco. That's where I met Paul Verhoeven, and produced *Basic Instinct* for him," Marshall notes.

After next producing the Sylvester Stallone–starring *Cliffhanger*, Marshall was set to produce Verhoeven's *Mistress of the Seas/The Crusade* before both came to naught. "At which point we did *Showgirls,*" Marshall picks up. "Now, I presume Jon Davison had already asked Paul whether he was interested in doing *Starship Troopers* prior to shooting *Showgirls,* because one day Paul came to me and said he wanted to make this extrava-

Early concept painting by Steve Burg of the Cap Troopers uniform. Note the "Jump Boots" on the female Trooper's feet; this was an early effort to visualize "The Bounce" mentioned in Robert A. Heinlein's novel. "The Bounce," however, was never filmed.

Inside ST's wardrobe warehouse [opposite], a worker attends to one of the hundreds of futuristic military helmets manufactured for the film. [Inset] Jim Martin's preliminary painting of an MI warrior housed within a Drop Ship "Trooper Stall."

Casper Van Dien, James Morse, Dina Meyer and Seth Gilliam fight a Bug on Tango Urilla.

gant science fiction film. But Paul also said he'd like me to be part of his side of the deal. I examined the project and was intrigued by Paul and Ed's respect for the actual story line of *Starship Troopers;* both of them insisted we not forgo the story just because we were going to make a film about people fighting bugs.

"In a film like *Starship Troopers,* one actually could have forgone any sort of coherent plot and just gone for the spectacular. However, to our mutual way of thinking, if you didn't like *ST*'s characters, then the film was going to fall into that category of 'all spectacle but no substance.' Luckily, at this time we stand a good chance of having the audience falling in love with our characters. That's what's strong about this script. And refreshing. There's no point in going to this movie and introducing the audience to a gang of young kids fighting huge bugs unless you actually care about the kids who are doing the fighting."

Promising script or not, Marshall soon found himself facing the same *ST* obstacle which was frustrating Jon Davison. "It was money," the bearded, no-nonsense producer flatly states. "We'd determined from the start that this was going to be an expensive movie to make—a very expensive movie. There simply wasn't any other way to get Heinlein's novel onto the screen. And frankly, I wasn't happy with the original budget estimates that were submitted—I thought them unrealistic. Consequently, the major complaint we raised throughout production always came back to the same thing—funds. Not having enough funding to properly do our picture was an ongoing concern with *Starship Troopers*."

But how were *ST*'s administrative chores divided between its two producers?

"I actually like the effects side of filmmaking a little bit more than Alan, I think," Davison replies. "So I tended to spend a little more time with the special effects. Alan dealt more with the regular shooting aspects of making this picture. Although our functions did overlap."

"After producing *Pink Floyd: The Wall* and *Cliffhanger,* which both used every trick imaginable," Marshall himself continues, explaining his responsibilities concerning the "regular shooting aspects of the picture," "I am quite familiar and comfortable with special effects. So on *ST* I obviously was involved with them.

"But in daily terms, every question that was asked by every department during the making of this motion picture finished up on my desk. And every piece of paper that involved spending finished up on my desk. I had to approve or disapprove everything because we only had X amount of dollars to spend. Which meant that I had to sanction everything from how many toilet paper rolls we bought per week to how many lights were required to light a set.

"Having said all that," Marshall concludes, "my primary job on *Starship Troopers* was to produce the movie for Paul Verhoeven. So I tried to protect his creative juices and take as much pressure off of him as possible. That way Paul could get on with his job as a director, and not have to worry about the 1,001 other things that were happening behind his back."

Growth of the Bugs

Meanwhile, Tippett Studio was engaged in a frenzy of activity. A second structure had recently been acquired by the Berkeley-based company in order to augment its original, smaller one; this second building now housed the numerous computer workstations, digital F/X tools, and new employees needed to produce *ST*'s literal army of Bugs.

Paul Verhoeven's sketched vision of a
fleet ship flying through Bug plasma.

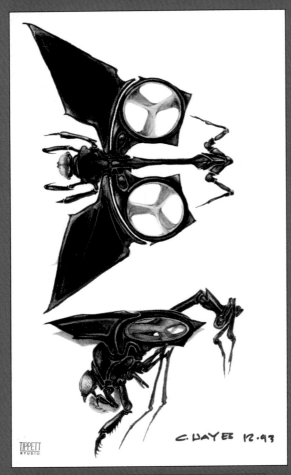

Craig Hayes' "bio-mechanical" Hopper design was eventually scrapped in favor of a more organic look.

Unused Craig Hayes concept for the Brain Bug.

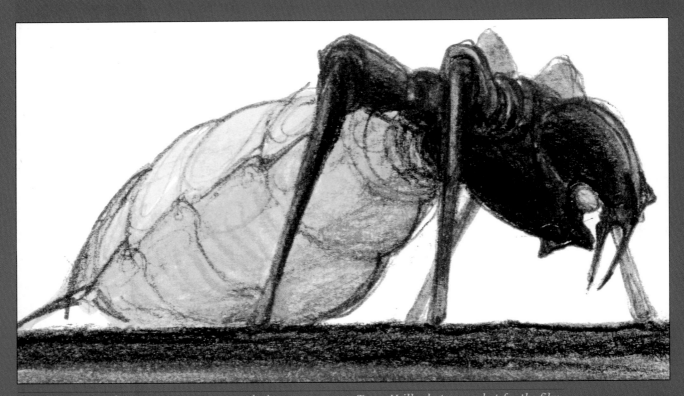

Craig Hayes' "Breeder Bug," meant to appear during a sequence on Tango Urilla, but never shot for the film.

KNOW YOUR FOE

REPORT ALL ENCOUNTERS WITH BUGS TO YOUR SUPERVISOR

WARRIOR: (UROPYGI)
* CDR: 1   550 kg   IQ: 30

Very aggressive. High agility in any combat environment. Exo-armor can withstand temperatures above 500° c. Low intelligence, excellent follow-through.

Weapons: Cutting/chewing mandibles. Jaws exert in excess of 4000 foot-pounds/kg
Ground speed: Cross country -- 64 km/hr Acceleration (0 to 50 km) -- 7.2 seconds

HOPPER (OPILIONES)
* CDR: 1 485 kg IQ: 30

Very aggressive. Jumping and short flight capability.
Weapons: See warrior specifications
Ground speed: See warrior specifications
Jump range: 50 meters
Glide ratio: 1-3
Air speed: Up to 341 km/hr

* CDR: 2   70 kg   IQ: 20

BREEDER (SYINGOPHILIDAE)
Aggressive when confronted. Piercing tail is dangerous at close-quarters. Specialized "activation fuel" for bug plasma operations is extremely toxic.
Weapons: Cutting/chewing mandibles
Ground speed: Cross country 35km/hr

BRAIN BUG (CEREBUS REX)
May be a very large insect, one metric ton or more.   * CDR: ?   dimensions unknown   IQ: ?
Believed to be capable of reason. May have intuitive and psycho-kinetic powers.   May be aggressive when confronted.
Weapons: Evidence of piercing type claw or palp   **Ground speed:** No data

WORKER (LASIUS NOIR)
* CDR: 3   500 kg   IQ: 18

Non-aggressive. Capable of lifting 10 times its own body weight. Ingests rock sediment and regurgitates cement-like substance for engineering purposes.
Load speed:
Cross country -- 34 km/hr
60% Slope -- 8 km/hr
Weapons: Claws and pincers are dangerous at close range.

PLASMA BUG (SOLIFUGAE)
* CDR: 3   7-0 metric tons   IQ: 18

Non-aggressive. Generates one-time only accelerated burst of high-energy plasma. The Plasma Bug is chemically stable until contact with the Breeder.

Can be fired ballistically or aimed with precision into high planetary orbit.

Weapons: High-energy plasma
Ground speed: Less than 2 km/hr

TANKER (AMBLYPYGI)
* CDR: 1   3.5 metric tons   IQ: 35

Very aggressive. Fast in tight situations. 1 metric ton bio-corrosive reservoir. Effective range of bio-corrosive is unknown but thought to be under 50 meters.
Weapons: Sprays highly bio-corrosive fluid
Cutting/chewing mandibles
Speed: Cross country -- 35 km/hr

CHARIOT BUG (SCHIZOPELTIDA)
* CDR: 2   220kg   IQ: 12

Non-aggressive. In large numbers they will stampede. The sole function of these relatively small Arachnids is to transport Queens and other large insects whose weight and function prohibits self-propelled movement.
Weapons: Cutting/chewing mandibles   **Ground speed:** 35 km/hr

FROM MOBILE INFANTRY DEATH FROM ABOVE

* COMBAT DANGER RATING

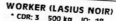

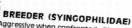
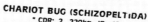

This early "Bug Chart" generated by the Starship Troopers art department illustrates the types, "danger ratings," and capabilities of ST's various giant insects.

"Scene 49" storyboard of a captured Warrior Bug eating a cow. Originally, this "FedNet" segment was scripted to include white-smocked scientists observing the Bug's behavior outside its cage; ultimately, however, the scene was changed to show only the cow being shoved into the Bug's holding pen by a "Cow Wrangler" (portrayed by Making of Starship Troopers author Paul M. Sammon).

SHOT#

(Hand held (CAM) PANS ACROSS LAB. INT.
CAGED WARRIOR BUG IS OBSERVED
By scientists - They move to Bars

MAR 2 6 1996   ①

*Craig Hayes' art
for the Plasma
Bugs.*

Additionally, a 1995 recruitment drive had also been implemented by Tippett Studio to help find those new employees (part of which involved the creation of two amusing STARSHIP TROOPERS NEEDS YOU! recruiting posters). By early 1996, this drive resulted in the hiring of almost a hundred additional staff members, many exclusively devoted to the digital creation of *ST*'s arachnids.

This "ST/Tippett team" was made up of old and new Tippett Studio employees: Tippett himself, Jules Roman (Tippett visual effects producer), Craig Hayes, Paula Luchessi (lead CG painter), Trey Stokes (Animation Department head), Adam Valdez and Blair Clark (animators), Julie Newdoll (supervisor of CG lighting), Brennan Doyle (lead compositor), Desiree Mourad (lead environment/camera match move), Joanne Ladolcetta (lead rotoscoper), and many more.

Each of these supervisors, in turn, had other Bug employees working beneath them. Not all were involved with digital duties, either; such chores as the sculpting, building, and painting of maquettes (small statues used as 3-D representations of F/X "characters"), the

*Craig Hayes' conceptual
art of the Brain Bug
cranially depleting an
unfortunate victim.*

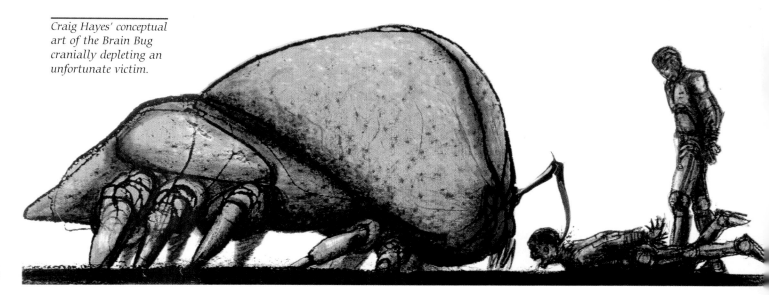

scanning of film into computers, and the handling of the company's various administrative/financial matters also needed to be addressed.

At the same time, Tippett and his LA-based colleagues were finessing the abilities of their computer-generated insects. "By the time Paul Verhoeven finished settling into his office on the Sony lot, we'd decided that the Bugs would not use technological weapons," Tippett explains. "Instead, they'd use their own biology as technology. A lot of that came from Paul himself, who felt that the Bugs would be biologically organized along the lines of military specialization. In other words, the Bug Rulers—whoever they might be—were capable of breeding whatever kind of Bug they needed as a *living* weapon.

"Once that idea locked into place, a lot of others followed it," Tippett continues. "For example, we came up with the Tanker Bug, this enormous burrowing beetle that sprays a corrosive organic acid. Another specialized insect was the Plasma Bug, the biggest creature in the film; Craig Hayes describes it as 'an eighty-foot cross between a volcano and a stinkbug.' The Plasma Bugs are these aliens' ultimate weapon. They can generate huge plasma charges within their bodies and spew that out through a sphincter into a planet's upper atmosphere, to knock an asteroid off course or to bring down a starship. So this idea of the Bugs using their own bodies as weapons led us to create a whole catalog of insects never mentioned in Heinlein's book."

Cuts, Drops, and Bounces

Changes between the *ST* novel and screenplay were not limited to new Bugs, however.

"When I first started writing this script," begins Ed Neumeier, "I gave myself the task of thinking that if Robert Heinlein were alive today, he would have read my screenplay and liked it. But bit by bit, certain elements of his novel dropped away. For instance, the original book mentions advanced canines called 'Neo-Dogs,' and features 'Queen Bugs'; those both were in my early drafts, but later seemed economically superfluous, so they were cut. Then there were the Skinnies, this other alien civilization Heinlein opens his novel with. Paul said, 'Let's not confuse things with two alien races; let's just make *ST* about Bugs against people.' Which I think was a good decision.

"Another element that went out the window—one we really tried to do—was what Heinlein called 'The Drop.' The Drop was Heinlein's method of futuristic troop placement. Each soldier was individually dropped into battle from an orbiting spacecraft, via a multilay-ered capsule that shielded them on their way down. In fact, it was this method of landing—Drop Capsules—that led to the Mobile Infantry soldiers being nicknamed 'Cap Troopers' in Heinlein's book. Well, we retained the phrase 'Cap Trooper' for our movie. But you won't see the actual capsules."

"Heinlein's Drop Capsules were jettisoned mostly for financial reasons," adds Jon

*An early Craig Hayes–
designed concept for
the Drop Capsules.*

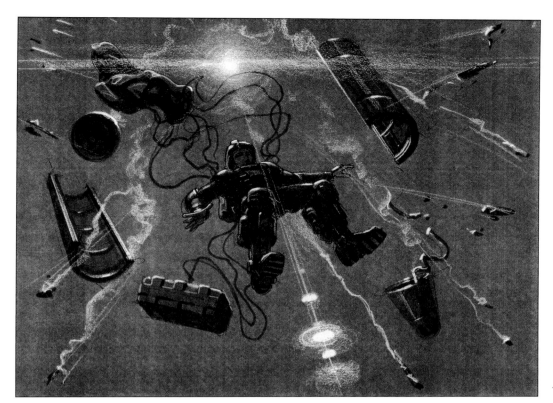

*Artist Steve Burg's
version of the Drop
Capsules suggested
they would separate
in a planet's upper
atmosphere, then
parachute MI
Troopers into combat.
The Drop Capsules
were eventually
jettisoned from ST for
budgetary reasons.*

Davison. "We did do some preliminary designs for those capsules, but the images that people initially came up with were pods equipped with parachutes for the capsules' entry into a planet's atmosphere, which really looked retro. Then we thought about firing braking rockets as the capsules broke apart, having the capsules separate into different sections with peeling skins as described in the book. But it all became enormously complex; to do a Drop Capsule sequence right would have required hundreds of effects elements and months of time. So we settled for Drop Ships, each holding dozens of men, instead.

"Economics also figured in our decision to exclude another of Heinlein's ideas we tried to keep in the film," Davison continues. "That was the Bounce. Heinlein had come up with hardware on the Troopers' outfits which let them, in effect, sort of jump up very high in the air, look around for a minute or two, and then fire down at an enemy before coming back to earth. Again, we discussed and scripted and even had paintings made of the Bounce. But again, this was a concept we couldn't fiscally defeat; we just couldn't afford to have hundreds of soldiers rocketing up into the air during a battle sequence. The Bounce also raised this question—if you could bounce way up in the air to escape the Bugs while they're charging you, why can't you just shoot down at them while you're up there? That would result in a massive Bug slaughter. So there was an artistic problem with that."

Alan Marshall chimes in with one more reason why certain Heinleinian-based sequences—particularly the Bounce—were cut from Neumeier's script.

"If we *had* gone with the Bounce," Marshall observes, "could we also have convinced an audience that this wasn't an army on pogo sticks? I mean, how would that work in a film? You'd have bouncing bodies all over the place, and I think Paul's concern was that that would never look real. So we removed bouncing from the movie. Instead, we've made *ST* much more like the Second World War in space."

The Power Suit Controversy

The most contentious excision from Heinlein's novel, however, involved what his book called "powered suits."

Also described as "powered armor"—but now generally referred to by fans of the novel as "Power Suits" or "Power Armor"—*ST*'s powered suit was originally portrayed as making its wearer look "like a big steel gorilla, armed with gorilla-sized weapons." Worn "like a suit of clothes," Power Suits were also equipped with infrared "snoopers" and multiple audio circuits, and gave the novel's Cap Troopers massive added strength.

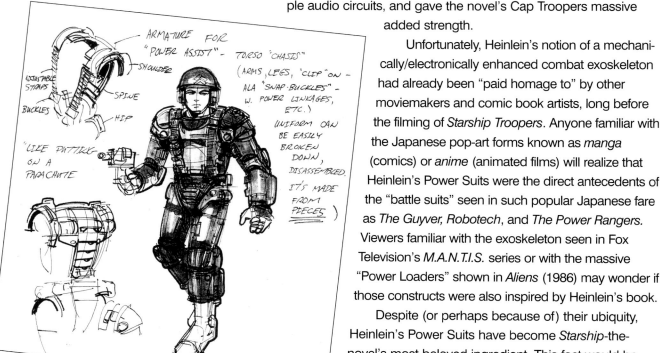

Unfortunately, Heinlein's notion of a mechanically/electronically enhanced combat exoskeleton had already been "paid homage to" by other moviemakers and comic book artists, long before the filming of *Starship Troopers*. Anyone familiar with the Japanese pop-art forms known as *manga* (comics) or *anime* (animated films) will realize that Heinlein's Power Suits were the direct antecedents of the "battle suits" seen in such popular Japanese fare as *The Guyver, Robotech*, and *The Power Rangers*. Viewers familiar with the exoskeleton seen in Fox Television's *M.A.N.T.I.S.* series or with the massive "Power Loaders" shown in *Aliens* (1986) may wonder if those constructs were also inspired by Heinlein's book.

Despite (or perhaps because of) their ubiquity, Heinlein's Power Suits have become *Starship*-the-novel's most beloved ingredient. This fact would be repeatedly brought home to the *ST* filmmakers in the months to come, as various Web pages on the Internet and/or outraged Heinlein readers attending science fiction conventions demanded to know why one of the most cherished concepts from "their" book had been dropped from the *ST* film adaptation.

"First of all," begins Jon Davison, "as a reader and an admirer of the novel myself, I was well aware of the importance of the Power Suits. And we tried to keep them in the picture—we really did. Again, we storyboarded them, discussed them, scripted them. But we immediately hit another dollar-based roadblock. I mean, do you have any idea how expensive it would have been to suit up hun-

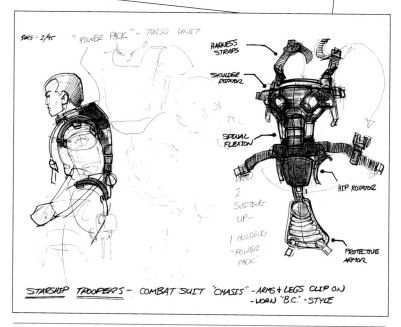

Steve Burg's 1995 never-filmed designs for the "Combat Chassis," a modified version of the original ST novel's "Power Armor."

dreds of extras and actors with those things? Plus there was an even more important question: What did we want this film to be about? Did we want it to be about Power Armor, or about the Bugs and the rest of Heinlein's book?

"Still, Paul Verhoeven and Ed and I wanted to come up with a workable solution to this problem. So what we initially decided was to just use the Power Suit *concept,* and sparingly at that. One of our ideas along these lines was to equip the Mobile Infantry suits with a few built-in weapons as well as "Jump Shoes" or "Bounce Boots," devices that could propel Troopers skyward during life-threatening situations. The crucial, underlying limitation here was that these Jump Shoes could only be used *once*—sort of like a contemporary jet pilot's ejection seat. But that concept dramatically complicated things. Because if a Trooper was going to go up into the air, he'd still be able to do a great deal of firepower damage to Bugs on the ground; it'd be like shooting fish in a barrel. Also, if we used this Bounce Boot idea once, then how would we explain why each and every major Trooper character in the movie didn't just jump away from his own hazardous situation? So that solution which addressed a budgetary issue didn't solve a dramatic problem. In fact, it reinforced it."

"Another major concern regarding the Power Armor," adds Alan Marshall, "was that everyone was frightened it was going to be illogical. I mean, if you're on the ground fighting an insect that's a great deal bigger than you are, but you can be mechanically enhanced to the point of being able to literally squeeze a Bug to death . . . well, all this extra capability means your jeopardy has been greatly reduced, doesn't it? We also had the horrible fear that hundreds of people bouncing across the ground or waddling around like metal gorillas was going to look stupid. Neither Paul Verhoeven nor I wanted to go to the enormous amount of effort and expense needed to visualize this concept just to have audiences laugh at it."

"It also eventually got to the point while we were scripting *ST,*" chips in Davison, "that if this film got any more expensive, the studio just wasn't going to make it. It was an enormous struggle to get this amount of money and crew in the first place—if we went back for one more dime, TriStar was never going to do it. So we really ended up having to cut things for political reasons, just to get the movie made."

"We didn't really have the time or the money to do all of the scenes I came up with," Ed Neumeier agrees. "But I'd like to think that the fans of Heinlein's novel will realize that our movie, at bottom, is the best advertisement possible for the original work. Let me rephrase that. What I genuinely hope one of the things this movie will do is to *get people to read Heinlein's book*!"

Cap Trooper Costumes

A much-respected wardrobe creator who has been working in the film industry since 1978, Ellen Mirojnick was *Starship Troopers'* costume designer. Mirojnick also costumed *Jacob's Ladder, Cliffhanger*, and *Basic Instinct* (all produced by Alan Marshall).

For *ST*, Mirojnick was joined by costume supervisor Nick Scarano. "And the first impression we both had about this picture was that its scale was enormous," Mirojnick explains. "Almost intimidatingly so," agrees Scarano. "I mean, obviously the film's militaristic wardrobe broke down into two basic areas—Mobile Infantry troopers and Fleet pilots.

But each of those two broad areas demanded additional sub-designs. Then we also had to provide costumes for the civilians on Earth, for the ruling Federal Council, and for the players on the jumpball game—to just name a few."

Ultimately, about 2,300 costumes were made for the film. Yet Mirojnick and Scarano initially employed only thirty staffers for the *ST* wardrobe department. "We didn't have the capacity to set up a whole shop, so our tailoring people primarily did wardrobe samples. Then we contracted out the work from there."

One chief subcontractor for the *ST* costumes was LA-based Proper Effects; by the end of production, this company had generated one thousand Mobile Infantry costumes, one thousand Trooper helmets, fifteen hundred Trooper boots, and eight hundred Trooper vests—all of which had to be constantly cleaned, repaired, and recycled during the actual filming of *Starship Troopers* itself. Each article of Cap Trooper

Craig Hayes' combination Drop Capsule (upper left) and Power Armor (right) merged both mechanisms into the same unit. Never used.

clothing was also unified by the same design philosophy—a philosophy which Mirojnick now explains.

"The Mobile Infantry uniforms—the outfits that *Starship Troopers* soldiers wear into combat—were obviously the single most important costumes in the film. So we started with sketches supplied by two artists who worked on *ST* during preproduction: Steve Burg and Jim Lima. That art was then radically refined by the input of Allan Cameron and Jim Martin, from the art department.

"Interestingly, the final approved drawings of the Trooper uniforms were pretty conservative," Mirojnick notes. "Especially since this was a sci-fi movie. But Paul Verhoeven

One of the best-remembered ideas from Heinlein's Starship Troopers *featured a high-tech exoskeleton called "Power Armor." While the ST production company attempted to integrate this concept into the film (as these two, never-realized Craig Hayes designs show), the "Power Armor," like "The Bounce," was ultimately deemed economically unfeasible, and was never filmed.*

always insisted that, yes, even though this story took place about four hundred years in the future, that didn't mean the Mobile Infantry outfits had to be all that futuristic. Especially after the Power Armor was dropped.

"Instead, Paul decided to make the Troopers' outfits more functional. So we began with the utilitarian, tried-and-true features found on most land-based battle gear: numerous pockets, heavy boots, solidly protective helmets, knife sheaves, that sort of thing. Allan Cameron then came up with the idea that the actual fabrics used on these uniforms could be a combination of woven nylon and polyurethane rubber, because that would give a soldier a great degree of body protection. Beyond that, the bottom line was any piece of equipment that these guys would carry into space had to work. And had to be real."

One particular item of the Cap Troopers' outfit, however, caused the Wardrobe Department no end of trouble. "That was the protective vest the MI troopers wear across their chests and backs," Nick Scarano explains. "Those had been designed as a Bug-specific type of lightweight body armor; the idea was, if you were going into space to fight an enemy that had claws, these vests would act as a protective covering. The problem was that even though these vests worked conceptually, the original design didn't work in terms of weight and practicality. And even though we tried at least four different versions of them, the final vests seen in the picture, which are also made of polyurethane rubber and nylon, may have been wonderful to look at, but they were awful to wear. We had to settle for them being heavy—about twenty-two pounds—and hot and uncomfortable."

Total weight of each Cap Trooper outfit, including helmet and vest, came to about forty-five pounds. "Still, the MI uniforms are very distinctive and visually intriguing to look at," Mirojnick concludes. "Which certainly satisfied wardrobe's concern."

Two unused concepts by artist John Bell illustrate initial ideas for the Mobile Infantry's field uniforms and weaponry.

The Boards

Despite the sudden rush of activity resulting from Verhoeven's now official relationship with Big Bug Pictures, the director himself had actually already spent several months prior to his arrival at *ST*'s production office "storyboarding various sequences of Ed's screenplay. These were my own boards," Verhoeven explains, "drawn when I had a spare moment during *Showgirls.* The reason I did so many of them [Verhoeven ultimately drew over four thousand individual *ST* storyboards] before we even hired an art department was because it was clear that if I *didn't* do that, I'd be dead.

"*Starship Troopers* was just too complicated. I mean, there were so many shots that were supposed to have Bugs in them, but in reality would have absolutely nothing in the frame during live-action shooting, since the creatures would be computer-generated later. So if I hadn't indicated before filming began where these CG insects were supposed to go, if I didn't have a plan as to how they were supposed to move within the frame, we would have been dead in the water midway through the first week of production."

Starship Troopers was not the first project for which Verhoeven had supplied his own boards. Although the director does not utilize them for every film—"I have no problem working completely free, without boards; it depends on the project"—storyboards were a natural outgrowth of Verhoeven's early artistic ambitions. "During my college years, and the first years I was a filmmaker," the director says, "I'd also wanted to become a painter. Consequently, I used to draw and paint a great deal. I was very heavily influenced by the Surrealists, for instance. However, I have since given painting up. But I still like to sketch."

Yet Verhoeven is pragmatic enough to realize "that I need storyboard artists on my films to make more professional drawings out of my sketches. Also, if I was constantly storyboarding, I'd never have time to direct."

Starship Troopers ultimately employed two storyboard artists. One was Robin Richesson, responsible for approximately 25 percent of the film's boards. The other 75 percent were done by one of the earliest crew members employed by the production: Giacomo Ghiazzi, hired onto Big Bug's payroll late in September 1995.

Ghiazzi provided comic book–like illustrations of *ST*'s various sequences for both the live-action scenes filmed by the first unit (the principal, or "first," team of filmmakers who shoot the major action of a film) and for Tippett Studio. "I did storyboards for Phil," Ghiazzi explains, "for the shots where the Bugs appear. These boards were very carefully coordinated between Phil and Paul, who really does his homework; Verhoeven had already done many highly detailed sketches himself, with camera angles and so on. My own boards were very carefully detailed in what they wanted for the Bug scenes. Because, of course, when it came time to shoot Phil's bug plates, there wouldn't be anything there in terms of monsters. Those had to be put in later, by CGI [computer-generated imagery]. So the Tippett boards were just as important as the ones Paul used for the first unit."

Paul Verhoeven's sketch of the Bug massacre on Klendathu.

Designing *Starship Troopers*

While Giacomo Ghiazzi's job was primarily to flesh out Verhoeven's sketches, the actual *design* of *Starship Troopers,* its overall "look," fell under the general auspices of production designer Allan Cameron.

Cameron had previously spent "eleven years at the London-based Thames Television Corporation, where I helped design everything from puppet programs to *The Benny Hill Show.* It was also at that company that I worked on such British made-for-TV films as *Edward and Mrs. Simpson* and *The Naked Civil Servant.*"

Allan Cameron made the subsequent jump from British television to motion pictures by working as a production designer on such titles as the Ron Howard–directed/Tom Cruise–starring *Far and Away,* plus 1994's and 1996's live-action adaptations of, respectively, *The Jungle Book* and *Pinocchio.* All told, Cameron has designed sixteen films, including *Showgirls,* which introduced him to Paul Verhoeven—just as *Starship Troopers* was Cameron's introduction to filmed science fiction. "That's exactly one of the reasons I decided to do *ST,*" Cameron adds. "Because I'd never done a science fiction picture before. I was also flattered when Paul asked me to work on this film; Verhoeven could have hired any designer in the world to work on a picture of this scope."

What did Cameron's design duties on *Starship Troopers* entail? "Since everything in this film is set in the future, everything needs to be designed. But I'm not only designing a single world; it's worlds, really. *Starship Troopers* takes place on the Earth of the future, plus a number of other planets; Klendathu, Tango Urilla, and Planet P.

"However, the primary design difference between *Troopers* and other contemporary SF pictures, such as *Star Wars* or *Star Trek,*" the personable, white-maned Englishman continues, "will, I think, be a certain sense of reality. Everything I'm designing, from the guns to the classrooms to the uniforms, are based on a technology that we now know. They're not totally fantasized. Instead, the props and sets and costumes in *Starship Troopers* lean more toward the familiar. So audiences will recognize our hardware and feel comfortable with it, since we all can relate to the past."

It was not only contemporary, realistic designs which influenced the look of *ST;* as Paul Verhoeven points out, specific echoes of contemporary *cities* also managed to find their way into the film.

"Earth's culture as portrayed in *Starship Troopers* is a very cleaned-up society," Verhoeven notes, "where kids, instead of asking for drugs, are asking for a kiss. I mean, there is really no criminality visible anymore. Everything is pure. Everybody has uniforms. It's a very disciplined society, where basically people can say to each other, 'I love you.'

"The challenge was to visually represent that culture. So I began thinking about key sequences in Ed Neumeier's script. One that stuck in my mind, which is also in the novel, is the public flogging Johnny Rico has to suffer because of a mistake he makes during basic training that gets another soldier killed. Of course, in our film, such a whipping is what's called 'administrative punishment,'" Verhoeven says with a laugh. "But that flogging made me think of the harshness of present-day Singapore, where a young American citizen was punished so severely for a prank. He was whipped, too, with a bamboo cane. So there's certainly a correlation between the culture seen in *ST* and a society like Singapore, that tries to reintroduce public corporal punishment on the person."

Adds Allan Cameron, "The Earth of *ST is* a bit like the Singapore of today. People living there, although they are individuals, are very oriented toward society. There's no sort of antisocial behavior. There's no graffiti. There's no litter on the ground. So our future Earth is crisp and green, with pure colors. From there, it followed that the architecture on our Earth would also be very pure—very formal, and very manicured. In fact, throughout this picture I've tried to subtly suggest that the Earth of *Starship Troopers* is, in effect, a planetwide military base."

Of course, although he was in overall charge of *ST*'s production design, Allan Cameron did not personally draw every blueprint or conceptual painting needed to pin down the thousands of *Starship Troopers'* visual details. That task demanded the creation of an *ST* Art Department. At its largest, this was made up of two art directors, three set designers, one conceptual artist, an administrative supervisor, and two storyboard artists.

"Finding my art directors was the immediate priority," continues Cameron. "First of all, I was looking for talented persons I could work with or get on with who'd previously done this type of film before. Because at the end of the day, even though each art director would have a specific area in which they'd be allowed a lot of freedom, it would be me who'd design something; the art directors would make sure it got made the way I wanted it."

Within three weeks of joining *Starship Troopers,* Cameron had found two art directors who fit those requirements. One was Steve Wolff (whose credits included design work on *The Shadow* and *Steel Magnolias*); the other was Bruce Hill (*Virtuosity, Teenage Mutant Ninja Turtles 3*). Two other key *ST* Art Department employees were associate art director Bob Fechtman (*Star Trek Generations*) and conceptual illustrator Jim Martin, who, according to Cameron, "roamed all over this picture. Jim definitely had a major role in contributing to *ST*'s overall look."

Crewing Up

The variety within the *Starship Troopers'* Art Department only underlines the fact that most films are made collaboratively. As Paul Verhoeven emphasizes, "Making movies is a group effort. To claim otherwise, especially on a picture as big as this, would be ridiculous. Putting together *Starship Troopers* was like constructing Notre Dame Cathedral; thousands of people worked on it, but no one person can take credit for the final building."

Those responsible for "building" *Starship Troopers* do not have to suffer the same anonymity imposed on medieval workmen. Among the first to "crew up" were production manager Robert Brown, production coordinator Daren Hicks, and assistant production coordinators Janet Campolito and Lisa Hackler, each of whom would be entrusted with overseeing the day-to-day operations of Big Bug Pictures. Also among the first to be hired were production accountant Greg Manson, first assistant accountant Linda Azevedo, second assistant accountant Benjamin Adams, and payroll manager Kelly Fein, who oversaw the production's cash flow. Equally important were the daily labors of Stacy Lumbrezer, Linda Kohn, Robin Berg, and David Latham, the assistants to Paul Verhoeven, Alan Marshall, and Jon Davison, respectively.

Paul Verhoeven's sketches later came alive as scenes in Starship Troopers.

The foregoing *ST* personnel were essentially office staff, responsible for managing the operations of the Big Bug Pictures production suite throughout the nearly two-year period it would take to guide *Starship* from its preproduction beginnings to its release in late 1997. However, the bulk of the *Starship Troopers* crew—some of the hardest-working, most professional technicians in the film industry—would only toil on the film for an average of six to ten months. And a large crew it was. If one were to tally up *Starship Troopers'* various designers, special effects contributors, cast members, extras, postproduction personnel, and so on, *ST*'s final employment total would hover close to the three thousand mark.

Conceptual artist Steve Burg's production painting shows Warrior Bugs attacking Carmen (Denise Richards) and Zander (Patrick Muldoon) after their Lifepod has crashed into the Bug Tunnels beneath Planet P.

Obviously, naming everyone from that list is beyond the capabilities of this book. However, a *short* list of key creative/technical crew members who, by late 1995/early 1996, had been hired to work on the film includes: Jost Vacano (director of cinematography), Vic Armstrong (second unit director/stunt coordinator), Mark Goldblatt (editor), John Richardson (special effects supervisor), Basil Poledouris (music), Stacey McIntosh (construction coordinator), Karen Higgins (general construction foreman), Gregg Goldstone (first assistant director), Kenneth Silverstein (second assistant director), Peter Hirsch (second assistant director), William O'Drobinak (camera operator), Jim Grce (chief lighting technician), Anette Haellmigk (second unit director of photography), Gary Dagg (key grip), Kathy Blondell (key hair), John Blake (key makeup artist), William A. Petrotta (prop master), Dickey Beer (assistant stunt coordinator), Steve Newman (publicity), Stephen Vaughan (still photographer), Haley McLane (script supervisor), Robert Gould (set dresser), Rick Thompson (second unit special effects coordinator), Joseph Geisinger (sound mixer), Raul A. Bruce (boom operator), Aaron Katz (video assist operator), Jim Chesney (transportation captain), Rock Galotti (weapons coordinator), David Presley (second unit video assist), and Michelson Food Services (caterer).

The Cast

Crewing up for *Starship Troopers* was a relatively easy task compared with the job of tracking down the actors needed to portray *ST*'s youthful cast.

"When we first began casting, we looked around for big stars in their late teens to early twenties, because the majority of the principal characters in *Starship Troopers* fall into that age group," Paul Verhoeven explains. "But we discovered that either the actors in that area were already working or, more importantly, that they didn't really *exist* in that age group. Most of the really big stars today are already in their thirties or older. So we had to make a lot of our own stars."

In essence, this dearth of younger film talent necessitated that *ST* search in an area often ignored by big-budget motion pictures—television. But by bypassing the usual class distinctions which exist in Hollywood between those who make movies and those who "do TV," Big Bug quickly discovered that such melodramatic weekly series as the Aaron Spelling–produced *Beverly Hills, 90210* and *Melrose Place* were solid training grounds for younger performers. These particular series were also ripe-to-bursting with accomplished twentysomething actors.

ST's prime discovery was Casper Van Dien. A classically handsome young man born in 1968 (who somewhat resembles a young Robert Conrad), Van Dien was picked to portray the pivotal role of *ST*'s, square-jawed yet lovesick protagonist. In a sense, this was perfect casting—given his background, the friendly, unpretentious actor actually *is* Johnny Rico.

"My grandfather served during World War I as an infantryman," Van Dien explains. "And every male in my family, except for my uncle and myself, has been in the armed services since. I did grow up in the military, though. My father was a Navy pilot for twenty years. I also went to an all-male military school, graduating third in command and seventh in my class. There are other parallels between myself and Johnny too.

"For instance, in *Starship Troopers,* Johnny is the captain of his high school football team, and I was the captain of *my* football team. Rico goes into the military, and *I* was in a military high school. So the character of Johnny was very familiar to me. In fact, if I hadn't gone into acting, I'd always thought I'd become either a naval pilot, like my dad, or a Navy Seal."

While growing up in Ridgewood, New Jersey, at 243 South Van Dien Avenue (from which he chose his stage name), Casper was regularly "taken by my parents to see Broadway and Off-Broadway productions, which I loved. I particularly enjoyed *West Side Story,* and found myself being drawn to acting and performance at an early age. I also loved old classic movies—especially the Hollywood romances! American Movie Classics, in fact, is my favorite TV station!

"But I still finished high school and started college. Then—well, it's funny, but it was really my dad who's responsible for getting me into show business.

"One day I was packing my car to drive back to college when my father pulled me aside and asked, 'Casper, what is it that you really want to do?' I said, 'Well, I'd like to be an actor.' He said, 'Then what are you going to college for?' I said, 'To get military scholarships, so I can serve my time like all the family does.' Then my dad looked at me and asked, 'Why!?!'" Casper laughs, then continues, "I said, 'Thanks, dad!' unpacked my college stuff, packed up for California instead, and drove out toward Los Angeles that same day."

Once located in LA, Van Dien joined the Screen Actors Guild and found himself "doing a lot of TV show guest spots and commercials." Van Dien's first leading role was in the upcoming theatrical film *James Dean: Race with Destiny*. He supplemented his appearance in this true-life film drama with television guest spots on the likes of *Married . . . with Children* and *Beverly Hills, 90210.*

Through it all, Van Dien remained "a huge science fiction fan. I've always loved sci-fi movies and books. In fact, I read and watched anything to do with the genre in elementary school, junior high, and high school. I still read science fiction and watch it today. For

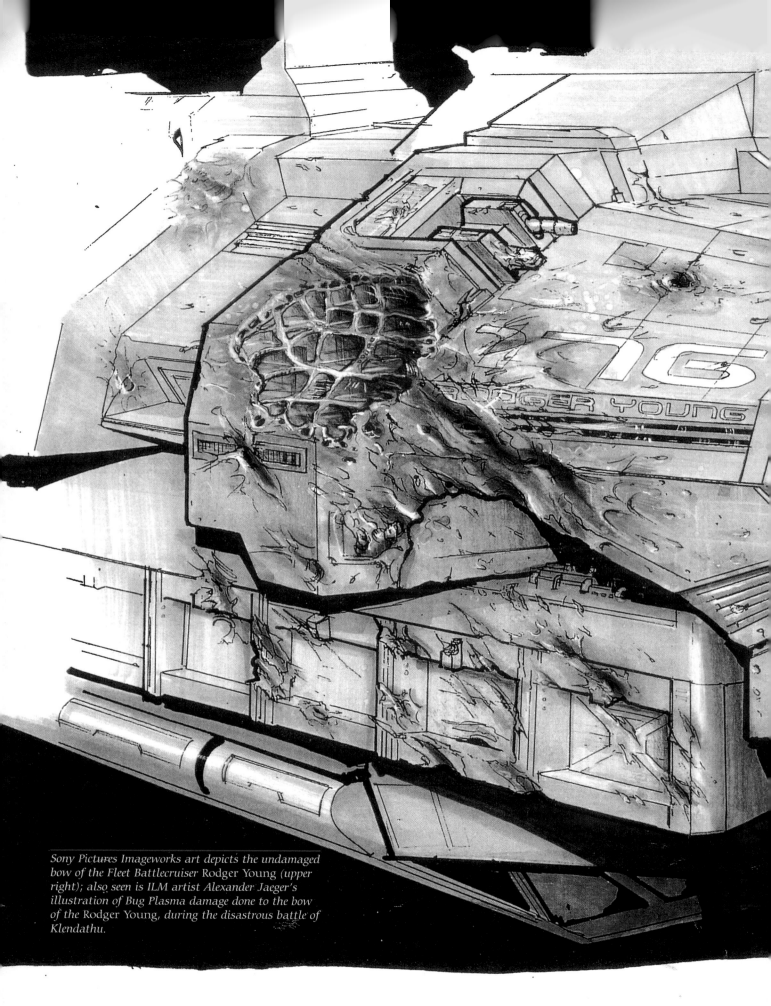

Sony Pictures Imageworks art depicts the undamaged bow of the Fleet Battlecruiser Rodger Young *(upper right); also seen is ILM artist Alexander Jaeger's illustration of Bug Plasma damage done to the bow of the* Rodger Young, *during the disastrous battle of Klendathu.*

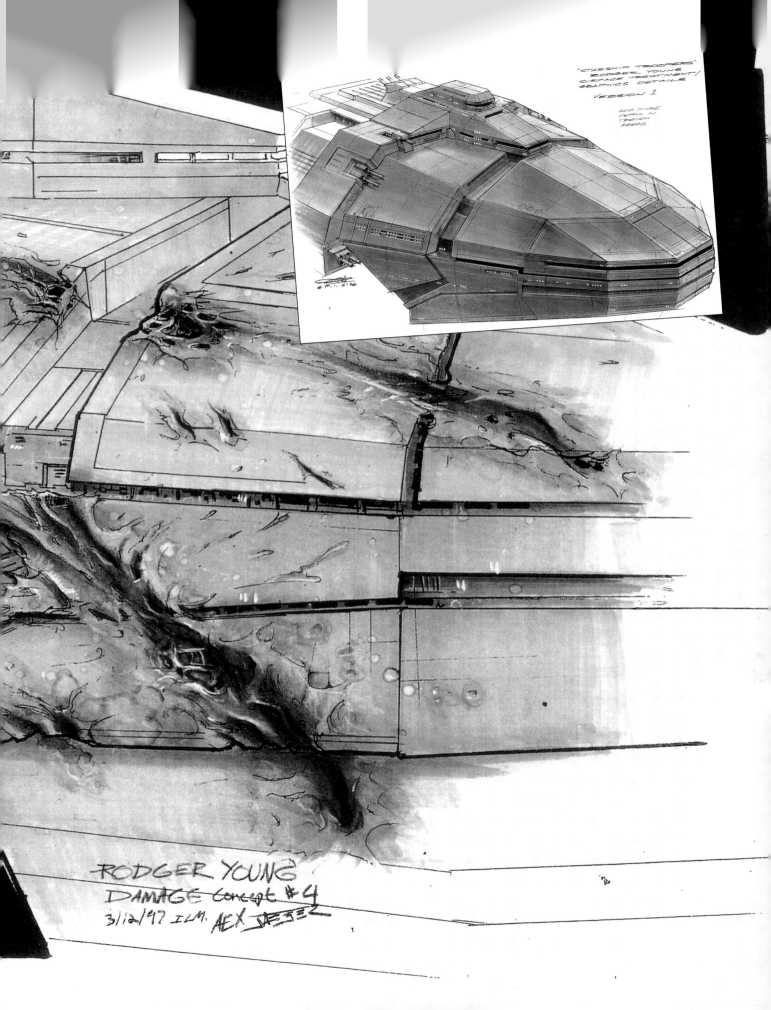

"STARSHIP TROOPERS"
RODGER YOUNG
SURFACE TREATMENT/
GRAPHICS DETAILS

VERSION 1

ADD MORE
DETAIL IN
TRENCH
AREAS.

RODGER YOUNG
DAMAGE Concept #4
3/12/97 ILM. AEX JESSEL

instance, I was a big *Star Wars* fan, I still try to catch the Sci-Fi Channel, and when I was a little kid I even collected *Star Trek* action figures. My favorite," the personable young actor adds, laughing, "was Captain Kirk.

"So getting a part in *Starship Troopers* is truly unbelievable to me," Van Dien enthuses. "Because I'd also read and was a huge fan of Robert Heinlein's novel when I was young. I just loved that book. And even though it took me five tries to get this part, now I'm Johnny Rico! It almost seems like a dream."

Johnny's love interest—the darkly beautiful, career-oriented Fleet pilot Carmen Ibanez—is portrayed by Denise Richards. Born in Illinois, the warm, sweet-natured Richards settled in San Diego when she was in her early teens, then moved to Los Angeles. Following her graduation from high school, she became a model for the highly regarded Elite Agency, with whom she spent two years doing fashion and runway modeling in New York, Los Angeles, and Tokyo.

"But I don't like to stress the fact that I was a model-turned-actress," Richards emphasizes. "Because ever since I was a little girl, I've wanted to act. I started seriously studying acting in high school, in fact, and continued to take acting classes in Los Angeles. I even cut my modeling career short because of my true passion. Really, acting has been all I've ever wanted to do."

Richards turned to full-time performing by "first doing small guest parts on television and appearances in commercials, to begin building my resume. I then guest-starred in a lot of other shows, did some TV movies like *In the Blink of an Eye* with Mimi Rogers and Veronica Hamel, was in a short-lived series called *Against the Grain*, and appeared in a lot of unsold TV pilots. I also worked with Patrick Muldoon, who plays Zander in *Starship Troopers*, on *Melrose Place* early in 1996. So basically, I've been very lucky. I decided to work full time as an actress about five years ago—so far, that's exactly what I've been doing."

Richards does admit, however, that her string of career breaks was sorely tested when it came to landing the part of Carmen Ibanez. "I first auditioned for Carmen in November of 1995," the actor recalls. "Then, nothing. Didn't hear anything for a month. Later I got

ILM Art Department supervisor Alexander Jaeger's conceptual illustration of ST's "Fleet Trainer," piloted by Carmen (Denise Richards) on a "wild ride" through the Lunar Ring.

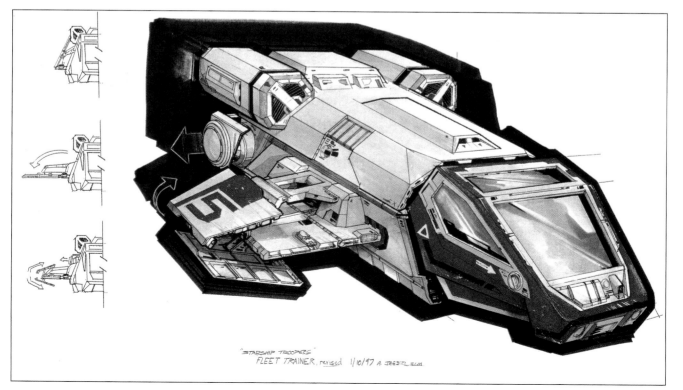

another call to read, this time for Paul Verhoeven. Again, nothing. Eventually, like Casper with Johnny, I had to audition *five times* before I finally ended up screen-testing for the part *with* Casper—and then we both got each of our respective roles! So it was a tough process, of coming back and really working hard to get this part.

"But that's how Carmen is, too. She's a very driven character—ambitious, focused on her career. Career is definitely what Carmen wants, before love or marriage. She even gives up a relationship with Johnny to pursue her dream of becoming a Fleet pilot for the Federal Service. Then, at the end, she finds out that she can have both career and romance. Which gives Carmen's character a parallel to contemporary women, I think."

One aspect of the role on which the fictional Carmen Ibanez and the very real Denise Richards part company, however, is this: "Carmen loves to fly—and I don't! I mean, one of the greatest fears in my life is flying! I'm terrified to even go *near* a plane!" Richards admits, laughing. "How ironic can you get?"

The third point of *Starship Troopers'* primary romantic triangle was filled by Dina Meyer, who plays the tough yet tender "other woman" in Rico's life, Dizzy Flores. Like Richards, Meyer "always wanted to be in the entertainment industry—or at least connected to it in some way. But that wasn't easy, because I had to fight for it."

Born in Queens, New York, Meyer realized that "as a child all I wanted to do—at first—was dance. So I danced, nonstop, for about ten years. When I was thirteen I was accepted to New York's High School of Performing Arts, which is very prestigious. But my parents didn't want me getting into the entertainment industry. They said it was too competitive, and that the chances of me being able to make a living at it were pretty slim. Instead, they wanted to steer me toward business.

"So I gave up dancing and started college in January 1986, to study business. "But after I graduated, I realized that although I'd enjoyed my college studies and what they'd done for me, business was not where I wanted to go. So I said, 'You know what, Mom and Dad? I know you are against this—but I have got to give show business a shot.'"

A woman whose personal characteristics mirror the "hard and soft" qualities of Dizzy Flores's fictional ones, Meyer began her showbiz career in the Manhattan-based television commercial industry. "Later, from September 1993 until February or March of 1994, I did about twelve episodes of *Beverly Hills, 90210,* playing a character called Lucinda Nicholson. That was a great experience. Then, a week after I'd finished *90210,* I was cast as the female lead in a twenty-six-million-dollar science fiction picture called *Johnny Mnemonic.* After I finished that, I pretty much went right into another big-budget movie, this one a fantasy called *Dragonheart*—which, by the way, featured a digitally created dragon created by Phil Tippett! So when I was asked to audition for *Starship Troopers,* all I could think was, 'Well, is this coincidental, or what?'

"But at first," the strawberry-blond Meyer continues, "my agent wanted me to test for the part of Carmen. Yet when I read the *Troopers* script, I connected more to Dizzy, because I think Dizzy's character is one of the most interesting in the whole picture. It would have been very easy to play her as a one-dimensional tough, but I didn't want to do that. I wanted to give Dizzy a heart. I wanted to make her vulnerable. I wanted her underlying love for Johnny to ultimately show in every scene, even when Dizzy's being the ultimate badass. Why? Because Dizzy has been in love with Johnny for a long time, yet has never been able to get really close to him. She's always been considered one of the guys, since she played this form of football called jumpball in high school with Johnny for a long, long time. Consequently, Johnny doesn't look at her as a woman. He looks at her as one of the fellas.

"So here," Meyer concludes, "was a tough, capable character who takes no crap from anyone, but also loves Johnny with all her heart, and would give him everything. Then she has to watch Johnny fall all over Carmen. I mean, how could I resist playing someone like that?"

Other, more seasoned film actors were also cast in *Starship Troopers*. These included Canadian-born Michael Ironside (playing teacher-turned-soldier Jean Rasczak), *Highlander*'s Clancy Brown (as supertough drill instructor Sergeant Zim), and Rue *"Golden Girls"* McClanahan as a blind biology teacher. Other key *Starship Troopers* roles were filled by Jake Busey (playing Ace Levy), Neil Patrick Harris (Carl Jenkins), Seth Gilliam (Sugar Watkins), Patrick Muldoon (Zander Barcalow), Matt Levin (Kitten Smith), Eric Bruskotter (Breckenridge), Tami-Adrian George (Djana'd), Blake Lindsley (Katrina), Anthony Ruivivar (Shujumi), Teo (Corporal Bronski), Ungela Brockman (Corporal Birdie), Brenda Strong (Captain Deladier), and Marshall Bell (General Owen).

ADI

Amalgamated Dynamics Incorporated was formed in 1988. A well-known special effects company based in Chatsworth, California, Amalgamated Dynamics Inc.'s credits include work on *Tremors, Alien III, The Santa Clause, Demolition Man, Jumanji*, and *Mortal Kombat*. In 1992, the company won a Best Visual Effects Oscar for *Death Becomes Her*. But what kind of special effects does ADI supply?

"Usually, full-scale monsters," answers ADI co-founder Alec Gillis. "Either complete props used for background purposes, or articulated figures controlled by mechanical and electronic means. Creatures capable of a wide variety of movements."

Amalgamated Dynamics was brought onto *ST* in September 1995. "Because," Gillis continues, "even if *ST*'s main effects emphasis was on Phil Tippett's CG Bugs, the production company knew they'd also have to employ someone to build a number of *real* Bugs. Full-scale props that could be used as set-dressing, or as objects for the cast to interact with.

"*Starship Troopers* turned out to be the biggest and most unusual job we've done up to this point. Not just in terms of the size of the full-scale creatures we built, but the total number of them. For example," Gillis continues, "we were contracted to supply two full-scale, hydraulically operated Warrior Bugs. These were equipped with sophisticated electronics that would allow them to do such things as move their bodies and pick up a full-grown man in their jaws; we named those Snappy and MechWar. Then we made ten dead Warrior Bugs and five burned ones that are seen during various combat sequences. All of those were full-scale and fully poseable. Each dead Warrior Bug had about thirty-four separate parts. All those had to be sculpted, scaled up from a maquette, molded, cast, seamed, and painted.

"We also did a section of the back of a Tanker Bug," Gillis continues, "that Johnny Rico jumps onto and rides during one part of the film. That was an enormous two-piece shell, mounted onto a rig designed by John Richardson, the floor effects supervisor on the show, to make that Tanker Bug shell buck and roll and shake and so on. ADI also delivered nine Arkellian Sand Beetles, extraterrestrial insects that are used for dissecting purposes in a high school biology lab. Finally, there was the Brain Bug. That's one of the key insects in the movie—it's sort of this 'Overmind' creature that controls all the other Bugs. We built a full-scale operable Brain Bug puppet head, too."

A total of seventy ADI workers were used to construct *Starship Troopers* props. Among these employees were such key personnel as Yuri Everson, ADI's on-set coordinator/supervisor who, as Tom Woodruff, ADI's other cofounder, points out, "worked closely with Alec Gillis to ensure that our creations were working properly on the *Starship Troopers* set. Yuri also was the interface between our entire mechanical effects crew, Paul Verhoeven, and *ST*'s assistant directors. That meant Yuri was there any day that either the first or second unit was filming one of ADI's creations.

"However," Woodruff continues, "we at ADI like to think that everyone in our company is equally important. George Bernota, who is our chief mechanical designer, spent probably as much time working out the controlling mechanisms for the mechanical warriors as he did on the Brain Bug, and did a great job on both. We also had this terrific painting team who studied the Bug maquettes Phil Tippett sent down for us to look at: Dan Brodzik, Kevin Marks, James Conrad, and Mike Larrabee translated the colors and shadings of the original Bug designs and established a viable pattern for painting the full-scale insects. We also have a guy named Steve Rosenbluth, who writes our software, to help control the electronics installed in our creations. Plus there were people who helped out on the *ST* set every day, like Steve Buscaino. I could go on and on."

"It's funny," Alec Gillis concludes, "When I was a kid, I was afraid of monsters. Now I'm afraid of just not getting them done on time!"

Imageworks, Locations, and the End of Prep

At the same time *Starship Troopers'* actors and shooting crew were assembled, more specialized technicians were being hired to help with the production's broad palette of special effects. Chief among these vendors were Kevin Yagher Productions Inc., supplier of *ST*'s prosthetic makeups, and Peter Kuran's Visual Concepts Engineering (VCE), which would contribute a variety of digital and animated F/X.

Yet *ST*'s most crucial effects company (other than Tippett Studio) was Sony Pictures Imageworks, or SPI.

An in-house facility headed up by former Industrial Light and Magic (ILM) employee and Academy Award–winning effects artist Ken Ralston, Imageworks is the Sony Pictures special effects company, an across-the-board provider of miniature, photographic, and digital effects. However, despite its expertise and breadth of available technology, "We really didn't want to use SPI as part of the *ST* effects team," remembers Jon Davison. "Originally we had some other companies in mind. But during our funding negotiations with TriStar and Sony Pictures, it was made rather clear that the only way we'd be able to get financing on this picture was if we agreed to use Sony's in-house F/X company. So we rather reluctantly said 'Okay.' We then decided to break the special effects of *Starship Troopers* into two broad areas: Tippett Studio would provide the Bugs, and SPI would provide the spaceships."

Despite its apparent prudence in acknowledging studio politics, however, Big Bug would eventually come to regret its decision to use Sony's in-house F/X group. For now,

ST *matte painter Mark Sullivan's gorgeous art depicts one version of the moon-based Tereshkova Fleet Academy.*

however, more pressing concerns needed to be addressed—such as where to actually *film Starship Troopers*.

Neumeier's *ST* script featured numerous scenes taking place within barracks, spacecraft, and schoolrooms; obviously, these sequences could be shot on the soundstages of Sony Studios. A number of other key scenes, however, involved exterior vistas of alien landscapes. This factor dictated the use of locations far from the Culver City lot.

"I personally scouted about six different states looking for the locations for those alien planets," Allan Cameron recalls. "Bill Bowling, our location manager, covered many more places than that. But those were rejected—one of the things we wanted for *Starship Troopers* were locations that were unique, or hadn't already been done to death."

For a short while it appeared as if one choice might be Nevada's Valley of Fire, a starkly beautiful site. "But the Valley of Fire is a state park," Jon Davison points out, "and the environmental restrictions were such that we just didn't feel we could shoot there without damaging it . . . or getting ourselves thrown out of it. Also, it was our bad luck to be scouting locations toward the end of 1995, which was a period when the federal government seemed to be shutting down every couple of weeks. That looked like it could go on for some time, and perhaps delay our shooting and permitting process. So we just really backed off from the idea of using national parks or state parks, or anything to do with the Bureau of Land Management.

"This decision, in turn, severely limited our choices—some of the most spectacular scenery in this country is owned by the government," Davison continues. "Then Bill Bowling came up with a place located just outside the town of Casper, Wyoming—a really

A "test composite" by painter Mark Sullivan shows three of Planet P.'s moons matted over the skies of the Hell's Half-Acre filming location. Only a portion of the mountains here are real; the rest is a matte painting.

unique valley filled with colorful buttes and pinnacles near the Powder River. It was called Hell's Half-Acre. Once we scouted that, we all decided Hell's Half-Acre would be a perfect place to portray the exteriors of Klendathu and Planet P.

"Right about the same time, we discovered a second wonderful location, on the edge of the Badlands in South Dakota," Davison goes on to say. "This was a place called the Barry Barber Ranch, near the town of Kadoka, South Dakota. It had very little vegetation, smooth, undulating geography, and looked just as alien as Hell's Half-Acre. So South Dakota got to stand in for Tango Urilla, where Johnny rides the back of a Tanker Bug."

With these primary locations secured, plans were implemented to begin building major sets within Hell's Half-Acre itself. Chief among them was the "Whiskey Outpost," a futuristic fort used by the Mobile Infantry on Planet P. (and the site of *the* major set-piece battle against the Bugs). Therefore, equipment, building materials, and personnel were now duly transported to Casper beginning in late February of 1996; the Whiskey Outpost set was completed six weeks later.

At the same time, all other *ST* departments—such as Sound, Wardrobe, Set Dressing, and Weapons—were being staffed and actively set in motion. Yet even as preproduction neared its end and a firm start date was set—with the first day of filming officially slated for April 29, 1996, in Hell's Half-Acre—producer Jon Davison still harbored doubts about *ST*'s upcoming production period.

"Due to the studio politics that had been going on all this time, and the on-again, off-again nature of the financing—even though we supposedly had an agreement—I felt the plug could always be pulled on us at any minute," Davison elaborates. "In fact, I never really believed that we were actually green-lighted on this picture until the last truck carrying the last piece of equipment left the Sony lot and was headed on its way to Wyoming. Even *then* I wondered!"

Despite such lingering concerns *Starship Troopers* had indeed reached the point where it was ready to face the cameras. And unlike the never-ending psychological pressures generated during its developmental and preproduction periods, *ST*'s principal photography phase would prove to be relatively stress-free.

That is, if one discounted the grueling, ongoing *physical* demands . . .

Cap Troopers race through the corridors of the Bull Run prior to the disastrous invasion of Klendathu.

Casper, WY

Near the end of April 1996, the *Starship Troopers* company had

securely based itself within the rolling plains and small-town ambiance of

Casper, Wyoming. Big Bug set up its production offices at 851 Werner Court,

Suite 218. This was the upper level of a two-story office building, one soon

transformed into the various offices needed by Marshall, Verhoeven, Davison,

and the rest of the *ST* staff—a fully functional editing and screening room was

added as well.

    At the same time they were setting up their home base, those laboring

on *Starship Troopers* discovered they'd become objects of fascination.

Residents had not had a genuine Hollywood movie company visit their area

since 1968, when John Wayne and director Andrew V. McLaglen used

Casper locations for the action/adventure film *Hellfighters*. The filming of *ST*

began generating enormous coverage in the local media; cast members, in

particular, soon became used to friendly, outgoing citizens asking for auto-

graphs and/or snapshots.

PRODUCTION

While such goodwill was certainly appreciated, behind the scenes Big Bug was discovering that its primary Casper filming site posed a host of challenges. "Logistically," says Jon Davison, "Hell's Half-Acre was a difficult location. First of all, it was about forty-five miles from the production office and company hotels, which meant that everyone usually had to get up about 5 A.M. and then take an hour's drive out of the city just to get to the location and start the day's work. Secondly, there was the geography to consider. Hell's Half-Acre is a raw, undeveloped site, with very rough terrain. So first we had to establish our location base camp on the flat mesa overlooking the canyon that makes up Hell's Half-Acre—the same base camp onto which we'd have to transport dozens of trucks, tents, and trailers for our various departments to work out of. Then we needed to construct roads just to get down into that canyon.

"However, we were very fortunate in that Natrona County, Wyoming, which owns Hell's Half-Acre and runs it as a county park, gave us total cooperation in regard to that location while we were shooting there," adds Alan Marshall. "In fact, they helped subsidize the construction of our base camp area and the roads we had to grade simply to be able to get down *into* Hell's Half-Acre. Natrona County and the Wyoming Film Commission both bent over backwards to give us the freedom we needed to responsibly film at Hell's Half-Acre once we arrived.

"There were some logistical obstacles concerned with that location, though," Davison concludes. "For instance, we had to helicopter in some of the props and equipment needed for our Whiskey Outpost set. Then we found out, from the locals, that the particular spot we'd chosen for that Outpost was infested with rattlesnakes! So filming in Hell's Half-Acre really did become something of a military operation."

Yet the greatest Wyoming location obstacle would prove not to be geography, logistics or snakes (no one was bitten during the entire Casper shoot, incidentally, although rattlers were certainly sighted). What did become a constant problem was Hell's Half-Acre's perversely unpredictable weather. Throughout the roughly six-week period the *ST* company remained in Wyoming, they would encounter torrential rains, snowstorms, and wind gusts clocked up to eighty miles an hour—sometimes all within the same day. Indeed, one night while the production was filming "Tippett Plates" for the Plasma Bugs seen during the Klendathu battle, the entire company was forced to literally flee their Hell's Half-Acre location due to a sudden downpour and subsequent "wash out."

Such was the expertise and careful planning of those in charge of *Starship Troopers*, however, that only a few days were lost to the weather. This was primarily because a number of fallback "weather cover scenes" had already been worked into the shooting schedule. Whenever wind, rain or biting cold made exterior filming impossible, the company moved indoors to a local warehouse that had been transformed into a soundstage, where filming continued unabated on said "fallback sequences" until conditions allowed a resumption of exterior filming.

The Cinematographer

Casper's changeable weather also could have played hob with the film's cinematography. That worry, however, was obliterated by the decades-long expertise of *ST*'s director of photography, Jost Vacano.

A tall, lean, German-born man who is a charming mix of the serious and silly, Vacano is routinely numbered among the world's most internationally acclaimed cinematographers. For his first project, in 1960, he and German director Peter Schamoni traveled to Moscow to shoot a documentary. Vacano went on to lens many more documentaries, plus commercials and German made-for-TV films. His first credit as director of photography on a feature film was *Schonzeit fur Fuechse* (*Don't Hunt the Foxes*). Since then, Vacano has amassed over a hundred television and feature film credits, shooting such other pictures as *The Neverending Story, 52 Pick-Up, The Lost Honor of Katharina Blum,* and the acclaimed submarine drama *Das Boot,* for which he received an Academy Award nomination for Best Cinematography (and invented a gyroscopically controlled, handheld camera called the GyroCam).

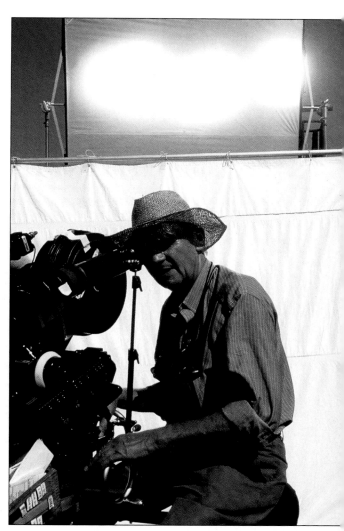

More to the point, Vacano has also been a longtime collaborator of Paul Verhoeven's, having previously shot his *Soldier of Orange, Spetters, RoboCop, Total Recall,* and *Showgirls* before *Starship Troopers.* My philosophy of camerawork," Vacano says, "is that movies are *motion* photography, not still photography. So this is one reason why Paul and I decided, for *Starship Troopers,* to use so much SteadiCam [a specially built piece of equipment strapped to an operator's body that frees the camera from its tripod and gives resulting shots a destabilized, "floating" feeling]. We feel it makes shots more fluid, exciting, and dynamic. Since *Starship Troopers* is really a futuristic war story, we thought SteadiCam would combine the best of the jerky, handheld quality of documentary combat footage seen in World War Two—which, in fact, Paul and I studied during preproduction: footage from the last world war of the Allies invading Japan—with a no-gravity, 'floating' quality, one that seemed equally appropriate for a science fiction picture."

Which explains Vacano's camera approach to *ST.* But what about the film's lighting scheme?

"*ST* isn't shot like *The Third Man* or something with dramatic, demonic shadows," Vacano concludes. "It's more a shiny, high-tech, polished world—antiseptic, almost. One with very saturated, very bright primary colors. Overall, the world of *Starship Troopers* has this clean, almost eye-catching look—which of course plays back to the statement Paul Verhoeven is trying to make about the human culture of this world."

Starship Troopers *director of cinematography, Jost Vacano.*

Plates and Stunts

Equally important to Verhoeven's vision of the world of *Starship Troopers,* particularly during its production phase, was second unit director Vic Armstrong. One of the most respected second unit directors and stunt coordinators in the international filmmaking community, Armstrong had previously worked with Verhoeven on *Total Recall.* Yet, as a young man, Armstrong, whose father was a race horse trainer, originally wanted to be a steeple-chase jockey. But after riding a horse in the 1965 film *Arabesque,* Armstrong turned to the world of motion pictures instead. By 1969, Armstrong had become a stunt coordinator, responsible for planning and supervising physical "gags" (as stunts are known within the industry). These assignments were numerous and far-flung—by his own estimate, Armstrong has worked on "at least two hundred films in forty-nine countries," whose titles have included *Ryan's Daughter, Superman, Terminator 2, Rob Roy,* and *The Last Action Hero.*

Vic Armstrong has also acted as a "regular" director in his own right (for the Dolph Lungren–starring action film *The Joshua Tree*). However, for *Starship Troopers,* Armstrong primarily served as second unit director/stunt coordinator. What did such activities entail?

"Well," the amiable, burly Englishman replies, "a second unit director oversees those shots or sequences which are basically too time-consuming for the first unit to shoot. Like complex stunts and/or special effects setups that, if done by the first unit, simply would stretch a film's scheduling resources to the limit. But the most difficult thing on this picture has been keeping my concentration up for the CGI Bug plates, which are shots that Tippett Studio will later lay the computer-generated insects into. These are very important, because they're such

Paul Verhoeven gives direction to Patrick Muldoon on location in Wyoming.

an integral part of the movie. The second unit will shoot just over a hundred of those plates, for later inclusion of Warriors and Tanker Bugs and so on.

"Yet this invisible plate stuff is very tricky. Not only are you framing the action for things that aren't there, most of the Bug plates have some sort of live element going on in them too, some sort of physical interaction that will make the later composited shot that much more believable. Like a barrel rolling away after a Bug supposedly jumps down off a wall and hits that barrel. Little things like that just tie the plate together and make the whole shot real when you watch it eventually in the cinema.

"So you must keep your concentration up," Armstrong restates. "Paul Verhoeven, in the early days of preproduction, said, 'Get the best plates possible to get.' And that's what we did. But that's also why I accepted doing *Starship Troopers* in the first place: I like Paul. He's extremely intelligent, very good at what he does, and makes some pretty unusual films. Great mind, great vision, that man.

"Of course," Armstrong continues "I was also *Starship Troopers*' stunt coordinator. Therefore, I had to advise what shape the stunts should take with Paul, and advise him on how things can be changed if I didn't think they were possible. I also hired the stuntmen; on *Starship Troopers,* we had at least twenty stuntmen at any given time, along with stunt doubles and what we call 'fall-down people.' Finally, since I directed the second unit as well, and filmed quite a bit of the action scenes, I needed to make sure that those scenes were shot interestingly and excitingly. Variety is important, because fights or action scenes can get very old and repetitive very quickly.

Assistant 1st Unit stunt coordinator Dickey Beer (seated, center, with white T-shirt) coaches Casper Van Dien's leap onto the back of a Tanker Bug during location shooting in South Dakota.

"However," Armstrong concludes, "since I was going to be directing the second unit every day on *ST,* I couldn't spread myself too thin. That's why I put a man named Dickey Beer in charge of the first unit stunts. Dickey is one of my protégés from twenty years ago, when he worked on *A Bridge Too Far* with me, his first film in the movie business. He's been with me ever since. And he's very good at what he does; I have full confidence in Dickey as a stuntman. In fact, Dickey stunt-coordinated some of Paul Verhoeven's earlier movies in Holland, so they already knew each other. And since they're both Dutch, they're on the same wavelength. What's more, they can *swear* at each other in Dutch, if they want to."

Boot Camp, Casper-Style

Within its first few weeks of arriving in Casper, the *Starship Troopers* production company had installed a local office, found lodgings for its employees, hammered out photographic and second unit strategies, established a large base camp at Hell's Half-Acre, and nearly completed construction of its principal Whiskey Outpost set. The first day of principal photography was rapidly approaching.

However, before the cameras could roll, one final detail needed to be implemented—sending selected *ST* actors and extras through a short but nevertheless genuine version of an actual military boot camp. This was conducted under the auspices of retired Marine Captain Dale Dye.

"I'd always been a movie fan—particularly of military movies, for obvious reasons—and I thought that Hollywood

Casper Van Dien takes a break between camera setups on the Camp Currie set.

did them very badly," begins the lean, rugged, colorful man responsible for training *Starship Troopers'* on-camera participants in the basic arts of warfare. "I just didn't see Hollywood reflecting what true soldiers are—what the true martial spirit is, what the true sense of public service is regarding the professional soldier. So eventually, around 1985, I thought, 'There must be a way to go to the top creative people in the entertainment business and say, "I can improve your creativity—I can make your performers

look and act and talk and feel like real soldiers. And I'll do this by training them as to what professional servicemen do."' So I came up with a company called Warriors Incorporated. I incorporated myself, brought in three or four others guys that I knew and trusted and who had been in Vietnam with me during my three tours of duty there, and then went around trying to sell my services as a military consultant."

Dye immediately hit pay dirt by becoming an official part of a production company "shooting this little film in the Philippines called *Platoon.*" For that subsequently much-honored, Oscar-winning motion picture, Dye created a three-week "actors' boot camp." During those weeks the principal *Platoon* performers, under Dye's no-nonsense supervision, learned basic combat skills; they also suffered through a short but intense version of the same type of "psychological deconstruction" impressed on thousands of new recruits on U.S. military bases around the world. *Platoon* director Oliver Stone (himself a combat veteran) then recommended "Captain Dye" to a whole host of other

Sgt. Zim (Clancy Brown) barks orders at Johnny Rico upon his arrival at Camp Currie.

Hollywood directors. The end result was that Warriors Incorporated has now trained performers on any number of motion pictures (including the 1996 Dustin Hoffman–starring *Outbreak*). Dye himself has also begun a secondary career as a character actor, appearing in such other films as Stone's *Natural Born Killers,* Brian DePalma's *Mission: Impossible,* and both *Under Siege* films.

"Working on *Starship Troopers* was sort of a special experience for me, however," Dye continues, "because I've always been a fan of Heinlein's book. I think I first read it when I was twelve, and I carried it around in my pack for years, as something I liked; I'd always seen a correlation between Heinlein's Cap Troopers and the infantry in the Marine Corps."

Dye then put together "a twelve-day syllabus, or training period, to take place on location at Hell's Half-Acre from April 17 to April 29, the first day of shooting. This syllabus was created for approximately thirty troops—six actors, twenty-four extras. It would essentially teach them today's basic combat skills and individual tactical movements as I perceived they would be four hundred years in the future, or whenever *Starship Troopers* is supposed to take place."

Dye's primary assistants in setting up and running his "Hell's Half-Acre Boot Camp" were Ruben Romo and "Michael Stokey, who is my gunnery sergeant. Mike was in my unit in Vietnam. We've known each other for thirty years and done a lot of pictures together." As for the *ST* actors who volunteered for this training period, these included Casper Van Dien, Denise Richards, Dina Meyer, Jake Busey, Seth Gilliam, and Curnal Aulisio (Sergeant Gillespie).

"I let it be known immediately that the Hell's Half-Acre training was going to comprise a

On Klendathu, Rico's (Casper Van Dien's) thigh is impaled by the upper jaw of a Warrior Bug. This shot required the combined special effects expertise of Tippet Studio, Amalgamated Dynamics, Inc., and Kevin Yagher Productions.

very physically rough and demanding syllabus," Dye continues. "For instance, I intended to keep everyone running about three miles per day, and make them do PT [physical training] every day to build their conditioning. But Casper, Wyoming, is also almost six thousand feet above sea level, and the air's very thin. You physically exert yourself and don't feel like you're getting enough oxygen. So I made it clear from the start—to the actors, to the extras—that this was going to be a tough regime. It needed to be."

Just how tough can be gleaned from listening to Maya Pruett (thirty years old) and Michael Ian Chizik (twenty-five), two *ST* extras who attended Dye's Wyoming camp.

"What Captain Dye asked from us was mostly commitment, and not to quit," says Pruett.

"Yeah," Chizik agrees. "Dye said it was going to be rough. That we were going to learn a lot of leadership-type things, and that we should be prepared to work hard—which everybody did—and that we should prepare to spend nights outdoors sleeping under the stars of Hell's Half-Acre.

"We sacked out under what the military charitably calls 'tents.' I called them 'ponchos on a stick.' Because that's what they were. Just two military ponchos, snapped together and supported over your head. 'Tents' with no backs or fronts."

"Psychologically," Pruett chimes in, "Captain Dye used what I would call the 'slap and tickle' kind of method. The bunch of guys he'd hired—Jim Morris, Pablo Espinoza, Joey Picata, Freddy Farnsworth—to teach us stuff like how to march, how to do maneuvers, how to handle the Morita rifles, and how to be yelled at—could be really harsh. And if you screwed up, they would make you do push-ups or other things. But when you got something right, they'd really pat you on the back—'Oh, great job!'—and build you way up. So everyone was at the same level. It didn't matter if you were an actor or an extra."

What did the film's primary cast member think?

"I'd done a modified form of boot camp ten years ago, when I was in military school," explains Casper Van Dien. "So doing it all over again, with actors and extras this time, out in Hell's Half-Acre, was fun. Really different. We did the physical training, of course, and learning to handle firearms. But we also did so much more.

"Like having to eat MREs. Good old field rations—which are really disgusting. Or raiding Bug holes and firing upon each other with blank ammunition, and running and ducking and hiding and covering and ambushing each other. We even had people quit because it was so hard, which is what happens in real boot camp and the military. So we got to have that experience, too; we got to know what it was actually like to lose people, whether because they were injured or just couldn't tough it out or whatever. That was intense.

"And the *weather* was intense," Van Dien recalls with a laugh. "For example, the first night we slept out there, we got hit with a blizzard—a *real* blizzard, with about two feet of snow and ice and everything. But everybody pulled together and got through that."

"However," as Dale Dye concludes, "Two days later, after the snow was beginning to melt and I was beginning to get back on track with the training, we had a windstorm blast through Hell's Half-Acre at eighty-five knots, gusting to one-twenty! Some of my little female Troopers, even with their body armor on, were literally picked up and set six to eight feet back. And we had to go catch them. It's no wonder that those kids are still talking about boot camp today."

One of these survivors was Julia Rupkalvus, an extra who became a key Dye assistant in training the hundreds of extras who would later portray Cap Troopers in the film. "Casper Van Dien was a hero. While some of the other people were in their hooches whining, Casper was out there in that incredibly bad weather with his gloves off, tying on extra poncho lines to our hooches to help keep us warm. I mean, he was out there working to keep all of the rest of us surviving! So he definitely won my heart that night."

A Short Digression

Reference has already been made to the sheer size and scope of the *Starship Troopers* project more than once in this book. As this book doesn't have the space here for a comprehensive examination of every *ST* scene, the following is an *overview* of *Starship Troopers'* principal photography, with short synopses of key sequences from the film. Special effects shots requiring extensive model work or digital photography—with the exception of Tippett Studio's Bug F/X, which set the tone for the picture—will not be covered here either. Instead, look to the Postproduction chapter for more information on the F/X labors of Sony Imageworks, ILM, Boss Film Studios, Visual Concepts Engineering, and Mass. Illusion Visual Effects.

The FedNet

Starship Troopers opens with an authoritarian "FedNet Announcer" promising that "Service Guarantees Citizenship." According to Paul Verhoeven, "The Federal Network, or FedNet, introduces audiences to the futuristic Earth of *Starship Troopers* by showing images designed to excite a population, images that are being narrated by an announcer who is very patriotic." This "Official Voice" also tells us that the Earth is being attacked by meteors directed toward our planet by the Bugs.

"The FedNet is not in Heinlein's book," Verhoeven explains. "It was invented for the film. Mechanically, the FedNet is sort of a futuristic, evolved Internet. Or a combination of today's World Wide Web and tomorrow's TV. It is the primary source of public information for *ST*'s future Earth. But the FedNet is not only a plot device; it's also *ST*'s way of predicting the eventual marriage between TV and computers, which I think will happen."

Mobile Infantry troopers ready their assault on the Planet P. Bug tunnels. The silver, half-cylinder–shaped objects in the foreground are actually small septic tanks, repainted and detailed by the ST Art Department to suggest futuristic storage bins.

Disaster on Klendathu

Next, on Klendathu, "a fierce orange planet ringed by an asteroid belt orbiting a double star, and source of the Bug meteor attacks," thousands of Mobile Infantry troops are landed in an attempt to stop the Bug menace dead in its tracks. But what begins as a heroic campaign turns into a military disaster. "I wanted audiences to immediately know what to expect from the battle scenes of this movie," says Paul Verhoeven. "That they could be disorienting, terrifying, and bloody, just like real combat itself. *Then* you get to know the characters, and how they arrived at this moment."

All the Klendathu battle scenes were shot at night, at Hell's Half-Acre, during June 1996. Between one and three hundred "Background Troopers" were used as extras each night. Eighty percent of *ST*'s opening Klendathu battle was shot with a SteadiCam, 20 percent with a handheld camera, to give this footage a jerky, "You Are There" quality, and to suggest that this was a live FedNet sequence being transmitted from Klendathu's surface.

Sugar Watkins (Seth Gilliam, front/center) leads a group of Cap Troopers searching the Planet P. Bug Tunnels for Carmen and Zander.

An Ethics Lecture

Following what appears to be the impending death of Johnny Rico on the insect-ravaged surface of Klendathu, a title card suddenly takes us back "One Year Earlier," to a small classroom (actually a set built on Sony Studios' Stage 23, and filmed late in July 1996) located within the "Buenos Aires Education Center." A lecture on what constitutes "a citizen" (which is taken directly from Robert Heinlein's novel, albeit in con-

Filming a "Bug Plate" for the scene of Rico, Ace and Sugar rescuing Carmen from the Brain Bug. Nearly all of the Bugs seen in the final version of this sequence were added during postproduction by Tippett Studio.

densed form) is being delivered by Jean Rasczak (pronounced "Rat-check"), a military veteran with only one hand.

Rasczak is played by Canadian actor Michael Ironside. A strong, distinctive performer born in Toronto in 1950, Ironside had "originally wanted to be a playwright before becoming an actor; I'd started by writing these little scenarios where I'd send my cousins off to Mars, or have them run over by big pickup trucks with lots of chrome." Ironside's feature film debut was in a 1974 picture called *Outrageous.* "But my part was cut out. And I'd already acted in about twenty subsequent films before I was noticed for playing the part of an evil telepath in David Cronenberg's *Scanners.*" Since then, Michael Ironside has lent his immediately identifiable presence to such other films as *Free Willy, Extreme Prejudice, Top Gun,* and *Highlander 2;* he has also guest-starred on hit television series like *ER.*

Ironside also appeared as a major villain in Paul Verhoeven's *Total Recall.* "Yet *Starship Troopers* was already familiar to me before I was offered Rasczak," Ironside recalls. "I'd read the novel in the sixties. I was also familiar with the way Heinlein set up the moral tone of his book early on, by that lecture delivered to a classroom full of high school kids. However, Jean Rasczak isn't in the book; he's an invented character for the film. Still, Paul Verhoeven wanted Rasczak, through his lecture and his asking of Rico to explain what a citizen is, to also be the one to set up the overall tone of the *ST* film adaptation early on."

Rasczak's Stump

"According to Paul Verhoeven, Rasczak had lost his mid-forearm and hand to some previous Bug battle before he became a teacher," says special prosthetic makeup supervisor Kevin Yagher. "So what my F/X crew did was to first cast a mold off of Michael Ironside's real arm. From that we made a clay positive, which we whittled down to a nubby stump that ends in a sort of triangular shape. That clay nub in turn was then cast up to arrive at another mold, into which we poured silicon, to make the stump itself. This final silicon nub was tinted flesh-colored, through dyes; punched through with human hairs; and painted by a Yagher employee named Thorn Floutz, who's really good at this sort of thing.

"The end result," Yagher finishes, "was a simple rod puppet stump. That was strapped into Michael by a shoulder harness. Ironside could operate the movements of that puppet stump himself by holding and manipulating a control rod in his real hand, which was sort of cocked out of the way behind his back."

Making the Grade

Exteriors showing Johnny and his classmates studying their final exam scores on a large outdoor TV screen were filmed at Kaiser Permanente Medical Center, in the Los Angeles suburb of Baldwin Park. The TV screen measured 7 by 10 feet, had been installed specifically for this sequence, and was part of a sophisticated device called a "Triple Light-Valve High-Definition Rear Projection System." This industrial-strength video projector is usually used at commercial trade shows and professional sports functions; it was provided by American Hi-Definition Inc. of Calabasas, California.

Biology Lab

The Biology Lab seen in *ST* was built only a few feet away from the Stage 23 set portraying Rasczak's classroom. Presiding over the dissection of "Arkellian Sand Beetles" during this Bio Lab sequence is another Federal Service veteran, this one a blind woman with dark glasses and a terrible facial scar.

The actress portraying this part was Rue McClanahan, best known for her continuing part as the sex-obsessed Blanche Devereaux on the long-running *Golden Girls* television program. McClanahan's facial scar was a gelatin-based appliance applied by Kevin Yagher Productions. The effect of which, coupled with the actor's dark glasses, white cane, and

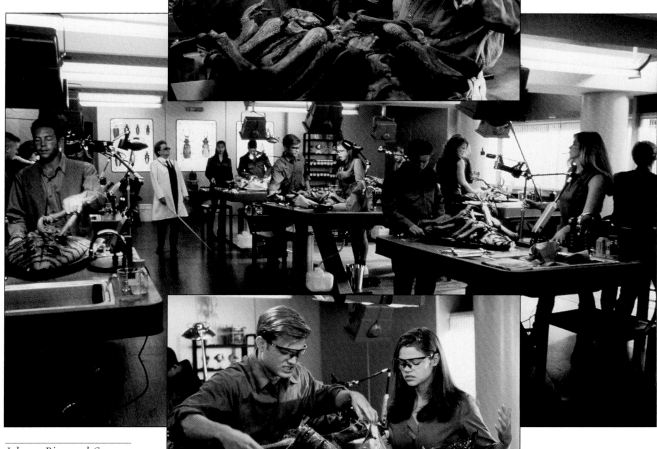

ST's Biology Lab, constructed on Stage 29 of the Sony Pictures Studio. The blind "teacher" (with white smock and sunglasses) was played by Rue McClanahan.

Paul Verhoeven (right) instructs Casper Van Dien on the proper way to dissect an Arkellian Sand Beetle.

Johnny Rico and Carmen Ibanez react to the (silicone and methacyl) innards of a giant Arkellian Sand Beetle, a prop built by ADI.

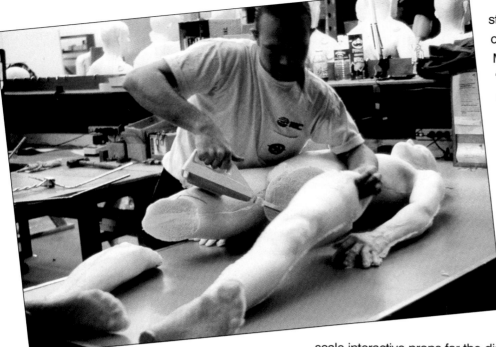

David Miner, of Kevin Yagher Productions, removes the leg from an unpainted, foam-core dummy that will ultimately serve as a Yagher "background body."

stern demeanor, led some *ST* crew members to describe McClanahan's character as "looking like a female Dr. Strangelove."

The Arkellian Sand Beetles dissected by the biology students were also the only Bugs in the entire film not designed or created by Tippett Studio. Instead, the job fell to Amalgamated Dynamics Inc.

"Since the Arkellian Sand Beetles were never going to be computer-generated, it was decided to let ADI make them as full-scale interactive props for the dissection sequence," relates Alec Gillis. "So first we did a series of sketches based on different insects like sand fleas and scorpions. But then Paul Verhoeven and I came across a real insect we both liked called a shield bug, and based the Sand Beetle shape on that."

Using a dozen separate silicone molds with fiberglass jackets, ADI cast twelve "positive pieces" for each Sand Beetle seen in the film; one head, one body, six legs, and various mandibles and spines. Nine Beetles in all were made, measuring three feet long by two feet wide. After being painted (and detailed with horse hairs), the primary Arkellian Sand Beetle body shell which Johnny and Carmen dissect was then packed with a combination of ultraslime and methacyl (two semiliquid compounds commonly used in the film industry for "slime" F/X), plus molded pieces of tinted silicon and foam latex to suggest the Bug's intestines. A thin plastic shell was then carefully placed over the Bug's abdomen, through which Casper Van Dien, using a real power tool, could actually cut while the scene was being filmed.

"Then I got to throw up," Denise Richards recalls. "All over the Beetle's intestines. On camera. They gave me something like creamed corn to hold in my mouth until it was time to do it. That was a career first!"

Carl's Basement

The sequence shot in the basement bedroom of Carl Jenkins, Johnny's best friend, was filmed on a specially constructed set built on Stage 29 of the Sony lot, after the *Starship* company returned from its Wyoming/South Dakota locations.

"Carl's a telepath who's just beginning to mature into his powers," explains actor Neil Patrick Harris (star of such TV-movies as *Snowbound: The Jim and Jennifer Stolpa Story* and the hit ABC-TV series *Doogie Howser*) of the character he portrays. "What he does during this scene is test Johnny's ESP on a sort of big video screen—and Johnny fails miserably. That was an enjoyable moment to shoot. Carl's pet ferret you see there, for example—that was a real animal. Very nice, highly trained. And though I don't think the camera ever shows this, the prop people who dressed Carl's bedroom left all these science fiction novels lying around as sort of an in-joke, to suggest Carl was a big sci-fi fan. Thing is, all those novels were real books . . . by Robert Heinlein!

"Carl's a guy who goes through real changes," says Harris. "He's bipolar, in a sense. Almost two completely separate characters. When you first meet Carl at school, in Buenos Aires, he's Johnny's best friend. A bit geeky, but also funny, with lots of energy and quips. Then Carl drops out of the picture for a while. When you next see him, he's giving 'practical lectures' (laughs) with a machine gun on the FedNet, showing how to blow a Warrior Bug apart! Which is sort of a funny moment. But then, when you finally see him again, it's after all these people have died on Klendathu during this horrible ambush. And now Carl is totally different. He's worn and pale and has the whole weight of the world on his shoulders. He's also dressed like a German Gestapo officer!

"So Carl's a fascinating character," Harris concludes. "Thanks to Paul Verhoeven, I've been given a great opportunity to show that I can play more than Doogie Howser here."

Jumpball

It is during a rousing game of Jumpball (a futuristic combination of football and gymnastics, whose game rules had been invented by Alan Marshall and David Latham, and was filmed within Long Beach's Pyramid Arena) that *ST* audiences are introduced to another key character in the

"All's fair in love & war"; Rico warns Zander to stay away from Carmen during the Jumpball Game.

Preproduction art for the elaborate "Jumpball Game," a futuristic sports sequence which had to be pared down due to cost and scheduling constraints.

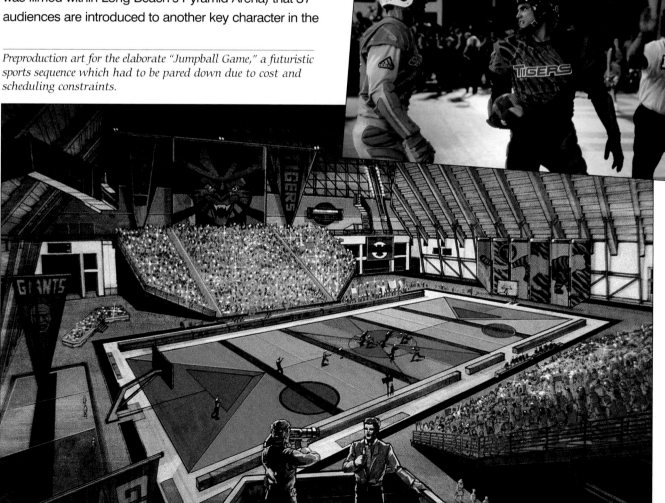

film—Zander Barcalow, quarterback for the "Tesla Giants," and Johnny Rico's major romantic rival for the attention of Carmen Ibanez.

Zander is portrayed by the darkly handsome Patrick Muldoon, who, with *Starship Troopers,* makes his feature film debut. Muldoon is no stranger to acting, however; he previously was a regular on the hit TV show *Melrose Place* (playing Richard Hart, a fashion company CEO), honed his craft during three seasons on the NBC soap opera *Days of Our Lives,* and guest-starred on such television programs as *Who's the Boss?, Silk Stalkings,* and *Saved by the Bell.*

"Zander Barcalow is an ambiguous character," says Muldoon, whose unaffected friendliness made him one of the most popular behind-the-scenes performers with the *ST* crew. "At first I think Paul Verhoeven and Ed Neumeier may have seem him as a bit darker person; he's very competitive, and he gets what he wants. But what we finally ended up with, I think, is actually a slightly tougher version of the relationship between Han Solo and Princess Leia in the *Star Wars* movies."

Before he became an actor concerned with a character's interior life, however, Muldoon was an award-winning college athlete, garnering two "Rose Bowl rings" as a member of the USC Trojans football team. "That's probably one of the reasons I had such a blast shooting the Jumpball scenes," Muldoon explains. "Casper and Dina Meyer and I did a lot of our own work during that sequence. I mean, there were some stunt people during certain shots—some *incredible* stunt people, who had to do flips and somersaults and things—but for the most part, that's really Dina and Casper and me mixing it up there. In fact, both Casper and Dina kept telling me, 'Go for it! Try to lay me out!' I was gobbling Tylenols after every camera set-up!"

During their high school graduation dance, a lovestruck Dizzy (Dina Meyer) asks a reluctant Johnny (Casper Van Dien) "why they never got together."

Prom Night

"During the Prom Night dance, Dizzy just about begs Johnny to pay attention to her," begins Dina Meyer. "She makes it pretty plain that Dizzy's serious about Rico. It's a great scene. Really romantic."

Over four hundred tuxedo and gown-dressed extras were employed for this night-time sequence, which was shot at the same Kaiser Permanente facility used for the earlier "Test Score" scene.

Student Enlistment

"The Federal Building, or Recruitment Center where Carmen, Johnny, and Carl take their oath of service the night after the Prom, was filmed at the Los Angeles Convention Center in downtown LA," says *ST*'s first assistant director, Gregg Goldstone. "Paul [Verhoeven] chose that location because he felt its futuristic architecture and spotless appearance fit right in with the look of our film's fictional Buenos Aires.

"We spent about three or four days there," Goldstone continues, "filming a number of different scenes. Some of them featured the largest amount of extras we had in the background for any interior *ST* shots. When Johnny sees Carmen off at the Federal Transportation Hub, for example, there were about four hundred extras there; when Rico and the rest swear allegiance to the Federal Service, about two hundred and seventy background extras were in that particular shot. And all of them were under the direct supervision of Peter Hirsch, the second 2nd assistant director, who did a great job keeping hundreds of extras pumped up and in character during the whole shoot."

"You really get a good look at the Federal Service emblem during the swearing-in scene," adds Allan Cameron. "That is a stylized bird on this huge green and gold banner at the start of the shot. Actually, Paul Verhoeven and I had a little fun with that. Because if you look at the Federal Service emblem closely, you'll see that we not only based this design on the American eagle, but made it more abstract and suggestive, by crossing that with a very warlike-looking airplane."

"[Then] when Johnny and Carmen turn in their papers to this Recruiting Sergeant, the actor who plays him gets a great line," continues Kevin Yagher. "He says, 'The Mobile Infantry made me the man I am today.' And the camera reveals that this guy has no legs, and an artificial steel hand! The actor playing that part really was a double amputee. But our F/X guys did his steel hand. Basically that's urethane, a type of foam. We made this custom urethane glove for him, then detailed that out with sectional pieces of another, harder kind of urethane to make it look like plated blue steel. Then we just painted it with metallic colors—instant steel hand."

Federal Transportation

Johnny later meets Carmen at the Federal Transportation Hub (actually the LA Convention Center), where Carmen steps into a Transporter Tube and is whisked away to a new life as a Fleet Cadet.

"The Transporter Tubes are a fanciful public transportation network, operated magnetically, that visually resemble the old pneumatic banking system," explains Bruce Hill, *ST* art director. "Some drive-up windows at banks today still have these small metal cylinders you can put your money in, drop into a tube, and then hear that cylinder being sucked over to

A quietly competent man with a wry sense of humor, John Richardson was in charge on *ST* of what are sometimes called "floor effects." That is, any special effect which occurs live, in-camera, during filming. In actuality, however, this innocuous sounding definition covers an enormous amount of technical ground: mechanical effects, pyrotechnic explosions, bullet hits, on-set electronics, special pneumatic rigs, wind effects, and much, much more. All of which, according to Richardson, "are on display in *Starship Troopers*. Plus a few new tricks."

British, and born in 1946, Richardson got into the film business through "nepotism. My father, Cliff Richardson, was probably one of the first effects men in England. He started in 1921, and supplied F/X for dozens of British and American pictures through the 1960s." Son John began his career by assisting his father on Otto Preminger's 1960 epic *Exodus*, the younger Richardson then struck out on his own in 1967. John Richardson's special effects work next received especially wide attention on two films—Sam Peckinpah's *Straw Dogs* (1971), and Richard Donner's *The Omen* (1976), for which Richardson created a much-talked-about decapitation effect. He has since worked on the likes of *The Devils* (1970), *Barry Lyndon* (1974), *Superman* (1977), *Willow* (1987), *Cliffhanger* (1992), *Broken Arrow* (1995) and five James Bond films (including 1988's *License to Kill*).

Very much a "hands on" technician often seen working on the various *Starship Troopers* sets, Richardson supervised a *ST* department of "about 21 people, including my chief assistants and helpers, such as Rick Thompson, Peter Albiez, Doug Hubbard, Wes Mattox, and John McLeod. We all had our work cut out for us."

Fellow Englishmen: Starship Troopers special effects co-ordinator John Richardson (left) and second unit director Vic Armstrong (right).

71

PRODUCTION

a bank teller by powerful pneumatic air-rams. Well, *Starship Troopers* elaborated on that. Allan Cameron and Paul Verhoeven enlarged the metal cylinders to a size big enough to house a number of human passengers; these travelers are then sucked away by magnetic force to their stops along the FTA (Federal Transport Authority) system of worldwide, underground feed lines."

Camp Currie

Cap Trooper extras wait between shots on the Camp Currie set, located in Fountain Valley, California.

The second stage of Johnny Rico's personal development, from popular schoolboy to military recruit, is set at Camp Currie, a Federal service training facility (taken directly from Heinlein's book). Finding a location for and actually building a real *ST* boot camp, however, was not as simple as imagining one for Heinlein's novel.

Begins Allan Cameron, "We finally settled on a place for Camp Currie in Fountain Valley, which is south of LA, called Mile Square Park. What I liked about Mile Square was that it still had an old, abandoned runway, one that had been used by blimps which flew out over the Pacific Ocean during World War II to look for Japanese submarines. That runway was in good enough shape so that all the production company had to do was lay down a top coat of fresh tarmac and paint in order to suggest a military parade ground. I also liked the fact that Mile Square Park was a flat area surrounded by a lot of green trees. That fit in with our original concept of a non-polluted Earth.

FIRING RANGE
CAMP CURRIE

Green "Target Grunts" were molded from plastic by John Richardson's Special Effects Department and were used during the Camp Currie firing range scene.

"In any event, it took us about six weeks to come in and transform this section of Mile Square Park into Camp Currie. First we graded the area, then poured out our black asphalt for the Parade Ground, then added seventeen buildings painted a drab olive color. Those structures were actually obtained from a company called Sprung Instant Structures; their buildings are completely prefabricated-type huts, from quite small to very large ones, made from a lightweight fireproof material which can be set up almost anywhere in a short amount of time. In fact, I used the same type of Sprung huts at the Whiskey Outpost set in Hell's Half-Acre, to give the impression that when the Mobile Infantry visited other planets, they just packed up their government-issued huts and took them along."

Besides its Parade Ground (which measured 150 by 150 feet), the Fountain Valley-based Camp Currie set also incorporated an obstacle course, knife-throwing range, war games course, and live-round firing range. Overall, Camp Currie's complete dimensions were five hundred by three hundred feet; up to three hundred extras were hired to "work" various areas of the camp in the background of different shots.

The Morita

Prominently featured during the Camp Currie scenes, the Morita is the standard issue rifle for the Mobile Infantry. It is also a totally fictional weapon.

"I named the Morita after a then-current Sony executive," Ed Neumeier comments. "As a sign of respect, not irony. The Morita's overall 'look' was also based on something real; initially, it was patterned after a Pancor Jackhammer. That's a genuine, futuristic-looking assault shotgun."

Producing functional Morita rifles involved the efforts of three different *Starship Troopers* departments; art, special effects, and weapons. "But the design of the Moritas was very much a cooperative effort," points out *ST* special effects department head John Richardson. "Which is somewhat unusual, because design is usually the sole province of the art department.

"However, I'd previously worked on a little picture called *Aliens*," Richardson continues. "And on that film, I'd been sort of responsible for getting *Aliens*'s weapons up and running—which were real firearms dressed up as futuristic ones. So once I realized that Paul Verhoeven wanted genuine weapons on *ST* as well, we used the knowledge we'd gleaned on *Aliens* in order to establish the fact that the Moritas would be real firearms hidden within manufactured outer shells. We then turned that idea over to the art department, to come up with the design for that casing. What they created was an over and under hybrid combining an automatic machine gun with a close range blaster."

Richardson next took that design and his own expertise "to a San Fernando Valley-based company named WKR, which has worked with me for years. WKR produced a number of Morita casings made from fiberglass. Of course, we also had to decide what real weapons we were going to put inside those casings."

On the Bug Tunnels set, weapons coordinator Rock Galotti (right) watches Denise Richards handle her "Morita carbine," actually a Ruger Mini–14 machine gun hidden within a specially constructed outer case.

That decision involved *ST* weapons coordinator Rock Galotti. A federally licensed professional responsible for the care, safety, handling, cleaning, and transportation of all of *ST*'s various firearms, Galotti is a former Marine and ongoing weapons expert with fourteen years' experience in the motion picture field; prior credits include such high-profile films as *Platoon, Born on the Fourth of July, Forrest Gump, Universal Soldier, Hard Target, Broken Arrow*, and *Face/Off*. "With the over-and-under configuration the Moritas dictated, we decided on using Ruger AC556 machine guns for the upper weapon, and twelve gauge Ithaca Stakeout shotguns for the one on the bottom," Galotti explains. "Of course, you just couldn't stick those firearms into the Morita casings and leave it at that. A lot of fine-tuning went on before that happened."

"First," adds John Richardson, "we decided to take the real weapons we were going to use out of *their* original casings and mount them inside the Morita casings instead. That was a lesson I had learned from *Aliens*; on that film, we'd used Thompson machine guns as the primary weapons, and had simply built a futuristic casing around them. But we'd had problems with that approach. So for *Starship Troopers*, we took our genuine firearms out of their shells and put them in the casings WKR built."

"Even though not every Morita actually had a shotgun in it, I still had to come up with a bracket that would allow the lower shotgun and upper machine gun to mount together and be stable inside the shell of the Moritas, which we did," Rock Galotti continues. "Otherwise, the weight of the shotgun would cause the barrels of the machine gun to bend. We also had to relocate the dual triggers up forward on the Morita casings, too, because the Rugers inside them have a rear mounted magazine feed. Then we made sure those casings were open for round ejection and ventilation. This was to aid in cooling; otherwise, since the real weapons inside them could heat up to 750 degrees Fahrenheit, the fiberglass Morita shells would've just melted around them. Finally we added nineteen-to twenty-two-inch-long barrel extensions to those fiberglass shells, making the overall length of the Morita barrels around thirty-two inches."

All told, Galotti, Richardson, and *Starship Troopers* used seventy fully-automatic Rugers, fifty semi-automatic ones (Ruger Mini-14s), and twenty-five Ithaca pump shotguns within certain select Moritas seen functioning in the film. Hundreds of rubber Moritas were also cast up, and used by extras playing Cap Troopers.

As for staff, Rock Galotti was aided in his *ST* weapons department by Christopher Davis and Manuel Baca. First unit propmaster William Petrotta and second unit prop department members Dwayne Grady and Ernie Lauterio "were also really helpful to us," Galotti points out. "And of course I made sure the actors who were going to be using the Moritas got in some good practice beforehand. We did a lot of training in Wyoming and a lot of training in South Dakota, for example; some of the actors and myself even got together and went to the Beverly Hills Gun Club.

"But what I remember now is the incredible amount of *cleaning* supplies the weapons department used for *Starship Troopers*," Galotti concludes. "I mean, we probably went through twenty gallons of MP7 Weapons Cleaner, approximately four hundred and fifty aerosol cans of Break Free Powder Blast, and three cases of Triflo Lubricant. You know why? Because we set off over *300,000 rounds* of blank ammunition on *ST*! That's a record for me. I have never, ever used as much ammunition on a film as I did for this one."

Sergeant Zim

During Johnny Rico's first day at Camp Currie, he and his fellow recruits are "welcomed" by the tough-talking, baton-wielding Sergeant Zim. "Who thinks they've got what it takes to knock me down?" Zim asks. An awkward cadet named Breckinridge (Eric Bruskotter) is foolish enough to accept Zim's challenge. Moments later, Breckenridge is

Sergeant Zim (Clancy Brown, right) tethers Johnny to a Camp Currie whipping post prior to ST's controversial flogging sequence, a scene taken directly from Robert Heinlein's original novel.

The "Federal Service" insignia at the center of the Camp Currie parade ground was created by ST's Art Department by combining a stylized American eagle with a war plane.

A pensive Dizzy Flores (Dina Meyer) broods over her unrequited love for Johnny Rico.

Rasczak (Michael Ironside, left) and Dizzy stumble upon a corpse whose brain has been removed at the Whiskey Outpost. Both the "head-hole" dummy and Rasczak's "steel hand" (actually a foam glove) were created by Kevin Yagher Productions Inc.

Dizzy's funeral, held in the Lifepod bay of the Rodger Young, is overseen by a grieving Rico (Casper Van Dien, at foot of coffin). Note the perfect alignment of the ranked soldiers. Such "geometric" groupings were director Paul Verhoeven's way of subtly linking ST to Nazi propaganda films like Triumph of the Will, which also featured rigidly composed crowd scenes.

gasping in pain and nursing a broken arm, actually a prop supplied by Kevin Yagher Productions, one with a fiberglass undercore and painted silicon "skin" (Bruskotter's real arm was strapped behind his back for this shot). Zim repeats his challenge, and a now just-arrived Cadet Dizzy Flores actually manages to knock Zim to the ground . . . before she too is subdued, this time into unconsciousness. "Medic!" Zim yells.

Sergeant Zim is portrayed by Clancy Brown. A 6'4" actor with piercing blue eyes, Brown is best known for his roles in such films as *Bad Boys* (Brown's first), *Buckaroo Banzai*, *Highlander*, and *Extreme Prejudice*. Clancy Brown is also, like Michael Ironside, an intelligent, well-read performer, quite unlike the villainous characters he usually portrays.

As for his thoughts on Sergeant Zim, Brown goes on to state that, "I love to read. So I'd already read a lot of Robert Heinlein before making *Starship Troopers*, mostly the work Heinlein did after *Stranger in a Strange Land*, when he was getting weird and fascinating. I read *ST* too, and was very glad to have picked it up. Because I really loved the character of Zim. You knew exactly what type of archetype Heinlein was writing about; the crusty, macho, jingoistic, ultimately admirable drill instructor. A real character. Purely American, and very cinematic. The gung-ho type you saw in something like *Sands of Iwo Jima*, or the kind of soldier Victor McLaglen used to play so well. So, in order to keep continuity with this classical movie character, first I watched an old film named *The DI* (1957), where Jack Webb plays what he thought it meant to be a drill instructor. Then I watched Lee Ermey do his brilliant job as a DI in *Full Metal Jacket* (1987). And I kept thinking about what Dale Dye told me one day: 'You have to remember that when you are a drill instructor, every second of every day that your recruits are in front of you, every second of every day that they can possibly see you, you are teaching them. Every action, every move, every twitch, even the way you look at them, has an effect.'

"But what I was finally trying to do with Zim," Brown emphasizes, "was to be faithful to this old American movie archetype of the tough-as-nails DI. So if somehow, someday, somebody mentions the Sergeant Zim character in the same breath as Victor McLaglen, I'll be in heaven."

When asked to explain how Zim can routinely break his charges' arms or suffocate them into unconsciousness during *ST*'s Camp Currie sequences, however, Brown becomes more thoughtful.

"I'm not sure if this is made clear in the final film—but in the context of this future world, a lot of physical injuries are fixable. I mean, in today's army, you couldn't stick somebody with a knife and you wouldn't break their arm, because they would then be out of commission. And filthy rich from the lawsuit [*laughs*]. But in *ST*'s world, those kind of hurts can be fixed in half an hour, at which point you can continue teaching the lesson."

Casper Van Dien strikes a heroic pose as Johnny Rico.

Ace Levy

Settling into his new daily routine, Rico soon forms friendships with other Federal Service recruits: Breckinridge, Kitten Smith (Matt Levin), Shujumi (Anthony Ruivivar). But since the world shown in *Starship Troopers* is blessedly free of sexual and racial bias,

Johnny also bonds with the female members of his Camp Currie group, women cadets who share equal military status—and the same barracks—with the men. These distaff warriors include friendly, red-headed Katrina (Blake Lindsley, both an actor and a trained opera singer), and Djana'd (Tami-Adrian George), a young black recruit. It is one final cadet, however—a tall, blond joker named Ace Levy—who'll soon become Johnny's closest Mobile Infantry friend.

"Ace starts out not liking Johnny and becomes really competitive with him," explains Jake Busey, son of established actor Gary Busey, who portrays Levy. "That's because he thinks Johnny's this stuck-up rich kid. Pretty soon, though, he decides Rico's all right, and they become buddies."

Jake says, "It wasn't until I was eighteen and attending college in Santa Barbara that I started to get serious about acting. Up until then, from the time I was seven, I'd been playing drums, and thought I'd probably wind up as a professional studio musician." Two years of acting classes in Los Angeles and a stint studying acting in Florida under renowned character actor James Best changed Busey's professional focus. He later began appearing in such films as *I'll Do Anything, Twister,* and *The Frighteners*. "The first time I was onscreen, though, was when I was five years old," Jake recalls. "That was for a picture called *Straight Time*, with my dad and Dustin Hoffman. After that, movie-making was pretty comfortable to me; I basically grew up around film sets."

Jake Busey (as Ace) fiddles a tune during a rare respite from his battle against ST's hostile Bugs.

Reflecting on the character of Levy, Busey states that "Ace, within the framework of *ST*, is an integral character. Because he's sort of a tension releaser. The kind of guy who, in the midst of a battle, can laugh. Ace can look at the worst things and find something hilarious and laughable about them. And Ace is kind of Johnny's right-hand man. We become friends, and look out for each other. But during the story, we also find out that Ace doesn't want to deal with the responsibility of becoming a leader. He doesn't want to have to worry about what someone else is doing. Ace is in the Mobile Infantry to fight and kill Bugs. Put a gun in his hand, tell him to destroy anything in his path, and Ace is happy."

Ace *isn't* happy, however, after questioning Sergeant Zim's wisdom of teaching an antiquated art like knife-throwing during a practice session on the Camp Currie "blade range"—since Zim answers by burying a dagger into Ace's palm!

"We made a prosthetic arm and hand for Ace in that shot," explains David Miner, responsible for many of the mechanics hidden inside the assorted *ST* prosthetics supplied by Kevin Yagher Productions. "We pulled a mold off of Jake Busey's real right hand and arm first, then built up a foam core duplicate with silicon skin and an inner mechanical structure made from nylon and aluminum. That moved the fingers, wrist and thumb. Jake Busey had his real arm strapped behind his back for the actual shot; our artificial one was attached to him by a shoulder harness, which was basically a piece of neoprene with a socket on it that we strapped to his shoulder."

Zim's knife was actually propelled into Yagher's prosthetic limb by a special knife-throwing device engineered by John Richardson. Resembling nothing more than an over-sized slingshot manufactured from steel and rubber surgical tubing, Richardson's construct was equipped with a grooved "guidance system" and a laser-based sighting arrangement, allowing any knife launched from it to unerringly hit exactly the same spot time and again.

The Showers

The one scene which perhaps best emphasizes *Starship Troopers'* presentation of a non-sexist, egalitarian future is the Camp Currie "Shower Sequence," during which male

This spectacular shot highlights the "Monitor Art" provided by Banned From the Ranch; the exploding ship is a Sony Pictures Imageworks model/miniature pyrotechnic effect.

MONITOR GRAPHICS

Starship Troopers' "monitor art" was primarily the contribution of Banned From the Ranch Entertainment (BFtR). "We sort of consider ourselves a visioning service," says BFtR computer graphics supervisor Van Ling. "Though some of the previous shows we've done, like *Twister, Congo,* and *The Relic,* were definitely big ones, it's been *Starship Troopers* that's given those in our company—our CG producer, Casey Cannon, our lead digital artist, Christopher "Sage" Greco, digital artists Allen Manning, Erich Ippen, and myself—the really unique opportunity to stretch the parameters of that service."

Along with CG coordinator Gail Wise, graphics editor Lauryl Duplechan, and Banned From the Ranch technical supervisor John Lima—whose crucial responsibility it was to be on the *Starship Troopers'* soundstages any time BFtR imagery was featured in a shot—Banned From the Ranch provided *ST* with computer graphics, video graphics, and even the text styles seen during the Federal Network sequences. But, as John Lima relates, "The graphics we did for the *Rodger Young* bridge scenes were probably the most visually arresting. I mean, there were about nine functioning computer monitors on that set, and BFtR did an average of three to four graphics per monitor. Plus there were different graphics constantly coming up for every scene showing the hero monitors in front of Carmen and Zander, the ones the camera was always looking at, graphics showing them trying to track an asteroid, warping into space, and so on. We did at least four dozen different graphics just for the *Rodger Young* bridge sequences alone."

Funneling those graphics into *ST*'s on-set monitors, however, was chiefly the domain of Scott M. Warner and Robert Chartier of Shockwave Entertainment, another professional video graphics company (which had previously lent its services to the likes of *True Lies, Terminator 2,* and *Independence Day*). "Our company's main responsibility," says Chartier, "involved the mechanical playback of various graphics during filming. And the way that worked was kind of interesting. Basically, I would run the wiring from the set monitors to this central command post located off the side of each set that we called 'Video Village.' Video Village had its own playback equipment and monitors to keep tabs on what was being shown on the set, and an independent power supply. And although Shockwave had already installed a variety of different videotape decks there, Banned From the Ranch also supplied us with a number of computers equipped with twenty-four-frame playback cards, to allow us to digitally pump the video graphics onto the sets. That way we could change the data involved in each graphic—its size, color, speed—in a very quick and efficient manner, and make it interactive to a certain extent, even during a shot, if the director wanted us to. We only went with video playback when some prerecorded material definitely had to be in a shot."

*The Mobile Infantry surveys the burned bugs
and scorched landscape after the bombing of
Tango Urilla.*

On location in the Badlands of South Dakota, the ST cast and crew pause between shots featuring the charred aftermath of the Tac Fighter air-strike on Tango Urilla. Note full-scale "Burnt Bug" prop in foreground, built by ADI.

Two Warriors crest LA's much-filmed Vasquez Rocks during an opening moment of the Bug Test; although shot in 1994, the design for the Warriors deviated little from their "look" in the final film.

and female recruits bathe together—in the nude—with no hint of embarrassment or arousal. "But came the day we actually had to take all our clothes off—and we did!—everybody was pretty nervous at first," continues Dina Meyer. "I think we all initially tried to cover that up with humor; 'Hey, I'm gonna see you naked!' 'Yeah? Well, I *want* to see you naked!' You know. That kind of thing.

"But when it finally came time to do it, some of us were *still* jittery. Paul Verhoeven was just great, though. He really calmed us down. They'd built a shower set at Sony Studios, and Paul had us gather round him there with our clothes on—there were about fifteen of us, men and women—and he just said, 'OK everybody, first we're gonna clear the set, then we're gonna close the stage doors. After we do, get naked at your own pace. We're in no big hurry. Just relax. Take it easy. Your clothes come off when you want them to. This way, hopefully, some of the initial embarrassment will go away, and you won't have to deal with that when you're doing the scene. You can just worry about your acting, and not "Omigod, I'm naked!"'

"Well," Meyer goes on, "here's the funny part. Paul went away right after he gave us that little talk. He'd handled the situation so well that most of us sort of looked at each other and smiled and got out of our clothes pretty quickly. In fact, Paul came back about five minutes later with Jost Vacano, who was going to film us, and they walked into a room full of laughing naked people! By now some of the girls were even saying things like, 'Hey, I've seen men with bigger boobs than mine!'

"Anyway, then Paul made some remark like, 'See? I told you. It's no big deal.' So we all turned to him and Jost and said, 'Hey, you two! Why are we the only naked ones here? How come *you* get to keep your clothes on?' Well, Paul looked at Jost. And they both nodded their heads. And then *they* took *their* clothes off. Just dropped their drawers to their ankles and picked up their shirts and—well, we'll leave it at that! Basically, it turned out to be a very funny day. And very innocent."

When asked for the male point of view regarding this incident, however, Casper Van Dien simply smiled and said, "How did it feel to be naked around all those people during the shower scene? It felt wet!"

War Games

After Rico receives a literal "Dear John" letter from Carmen, informing him that she's decided to choose a career over romance (an ironic decision, since Rico had entered the Federal service primarily to impress Carmen—and because she had joined the Fleet!), the broken-hearted Johnny stumbles into an even more disastrous situation; during a target-practice session using live ammunition, Rico allows Breckinridge to remove his protective helmet. Moments later, Breckinridge is accidentally killed.

This "Live-Fire Assault Range sequence" involved contributions from a number of different *ST* departments. John Richardson's special effects crew, for example, was respon-

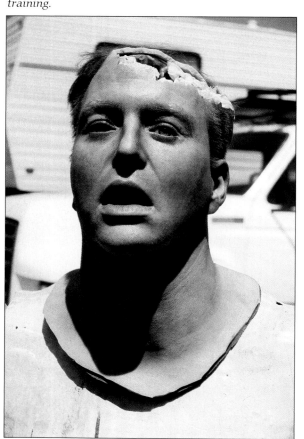

Kevin Yagher Productions' remark- ably lifelike "Breckinridge Head." Primarily made from foam and silicon; utilized for the scene where Breckinridge (Eric Bruskotter) is accidentally shot in the head during basic training.

KEVIN YAGHER PRODUCTIONS

"Prosthetic makeup" is a special effects discipline combining traditional makeup procedures with sophisticated mechanics and electronics. A simple example of this could be a thin tube hidden beneath a facial appliance applied to an actor's cheek, through which stage blood is pumped to simulate a bleeding wound. A more elaborate case might involve the construction of a lifesize, cable-and-radio-controlled dummy of that actor, to blow that character's body apart.

The Van Nuys, California-based Kevin Yagher Productions Inc. was chosen to be *Starship Troopers'* prosthetics makeup department. Hired onto the movie in December 1995, Yagher Productions is a busy and well-experienced company. It has provided such F/X as the "switched features" for the John Travolta/Nicholas Cage film *Face/Off*, the walking "Chucky" dolls for the *Child's Play* films, and the full-scale "Crypt Keeper" puppet seen introducing HBO's *Tales From the Crypt*.

"As for *Starship Troopers*," explains company founder Kevin Yagher, "we were called upon to supply a full range of prosthetic techniques. These included artificial metal hands, wounds, amputated arms, punctures, intestines, melted flesh, and elaborate half-torso puppets. But in terms of sheer quantity, the most important thing we had to produce were forty background bodies. These were various full-size male and female corpses—or parts of corpses, *Starship Troopers* being a Paul Verhoeven movie—that Paul intended to use as background detail for the battle scenes."

Yagher's alarmingly lifelike background bodies started as liquid polyfoam poured into human-sized molds, cast up, then carved and sculpted into full-scale bodies by the Yagher *ST* F/X crew (which at its greatest numbered twenty-eight). Individual limbs, used to portray arms and legs severed by the cruel claws of the Bugs, were also cast up from polyfoam; occasionally, additional limbs were generated by hacking-off arms and legs from the full-scale polyfoam bodies. All these props were then either coated or wrapped with thin layers of a lifelike silicone compound that eerily duplicated the texture of genuine human flesh. The final step involved head Yagher painter Thom Floutz's painting realistic flesh tones onto these silicone skins, plus the impressing of realistic wigs, eyes, and teeth onto each

Patrick Muldoon (right) meets his own head. This "Zander Puppet" was cast off the real actor by Kevin Yagher Productions Inc., then featured during the scene where the Brain Bug sucks out Zander's grey matter.

body. Various wounds and tattered flesh seen on the more mangled corpses were also composed of silicone, first molded and then painstakingly hand painted to resemble bloody, shredded human flesh.

Yagher's finished background bodies were constantly used, redressed, and reused for numerous sequences, including the grisly massacre at the Whiskey Outpost and the disastrous battle of Klendathu. A core group of Yagher employees were also on hand while the cameras rolled in order to ensure that the company's creations were kept in top working order. This onset Yagher crew consisted of the aforementioned Floutz, Yagher himself, David Barton (prosthetics/blood wrangler), Bryan Blair (silicon skin casting/general lab technician), Evan Brainard (mechanics/electronics), David Miner (puppeteering/mechanics), Shaun Smith (Yagher Productions supervisor), and Tony Acosta (prosthetics effects technician). Day-to-day activities of the Yagher Productions facility were handled by both Kevin and his brother, Chris Yagher.

"There are times when a director has sort of a gory scene in mind and hires you to create a makeup effect for that," Yagher concludes. "But when you bring your finished work to the set, that same director sort of flinches and goes, 'God! I didn't know it was going to be *that* gross!'" But Paul Verhoeven's not like that. He jumped full-bore into every prosthetic effect on this picture, gruesome or not, with total commitment."

Kevin Yagher places a foam-and-silicone "Decap head" atop an articulated dummy at the Whiskey Outpost; used for shot showing a Trooper beheaded by a low-flying "Hopper Bug."

sible for building forty man-sized, green, plastic "Target Grunts," futuristic bulls-eyes dotted with small explosive charges called "squibs" set off by Richardson's crew and capable of popping up from hidden pits on the Live-Fire Range (via pneumatic air rams). Kevin Yagher and company then manufactured a "Breckinridge dummy" for the moment when the hapless cadet has the top of his head blown off, after Djana'd's Morita rifle accidentally discharges into Breckinridge's face.

"The Breckinridge dummy was a full head and polyfoam torso we built and puppeteered especially for this scene," says Shaun Smith, Yagher Productions supervisor. "First we used a substance called dental alginate to pull a life-cast off of Eric Bruskotter's real head. Then we built a fiberglass skull for the dummy head, added glass eyes and human hair, and wrapped it all up with a silicon skin painted by Thom Floutz. Movements for the dummy head's eyes and jaw were controlled by mechanisms designed and built by Dave Miner, and operated by radio control.

"But for the actual effect of the top of Breckinridge's head coming off—which they shot as a closeup—we just attached a thin monofilament fishing line to a pre-scored section on the top of the dummy's head and gave it a yank. We also used compressed air to blow stage blood and brains out of the wound, once we'd yanked the top of the dummy's head off. And you could eat those brains," Smith concludes with an evil chuckle. "I made them mostly out of non-toxic materials: stage blood, methylcellulose, mashed bananas, and cereal!"

Administrative Punishment

"When Johnny inadvertently contributes to Breckinridge's death, he's given a choice—quit the MI or receive ten lashes during a public flogging. He chooses to be whipped," relates Clancy Brown. "That's a scene that's been transposed right from Heinlein's book. It's a core moment in the film as well. Not only for the formation of Rico's character; the flogging scene is also that intersection where we struggle with our humanism and practical natures.

"The other great little thing about Johnny being whipped," Brown continues, "is that it's one of the purest moments recapitulating the evolutionary and survival philosophies Heinlein put into his original book. What Heinlein was saying in his own flogging scene, I think, was that man is an animal. And that man understands pain. And that painful understanding is the best teacher—pain will direct the growth of a human being just as it directs the growth of life."

"A real whip is a very dangerous, lethal

First Unit first assistant director Gregg Goldstone (with cap) demonstrates how Casper Van Dien will ultimately be "strung up" for his Camp Currie flogging.

weapon," says Vic Armstrong. "Yet for this scene, we couldn't really use a stunt double for Casper, because the shot was so laid out as to be looking over Casper's shoulder and seem like that whip was really hitting him in the back. So the first thing I did was teach the actor playing Corporal Bronski (Teo), the enlisted man who actually flogs Johnny, how to handle a real bullwhip. That's a little skill I picked up doubling for Harrison Ford in the Indiana Jones pictures.

"Of course, the way we made sure that Casper wasn't injured during filming," Armstrong concludes, "was by first removing the tip of Teo's whip, and then by cheating our camera angle so that it looked like it was actually hitting him. It wasn't. The whip was snapping empty air a good three feet away from Casper the whole time."

A combination of special makeup appliances and digital effects tricks then contributed to the illusion of wounds appearing on Johnny's back. But what did Casper Van Dien think about setting himself up as *ST*'s whipping boy?

"As far as filming the actual scene went?" Van Dien concludes with a shrug, "I wasn't worried. I mean, I'd already been on this picture for months, and had total faith in the safety measures Paul and Vic Armstrong and Dickey Beer would take to make sure I got through that in one piece. Although I gotta tell you, it was incredibly hot the day we did that shot. So mainly, I just concentrated on getting a sun tan!"

Sony Imageworks director of model photography Pete Kozachik readies the top half of a miniature "Drop Ship" for filming.

Carmen and Zander's Lifepod suffers a crash landing deep within the Planet P. Bug Tunnels.

The Fleet Trainer

Meanwhile, a parallel *ST* story has been observing Carmen Ibanez's own military training as a Fleet pilot. During her opening Training scene, Carmen is seen racing another recruit down a corridor of the Moon-based "Tereshkova Fleet Academy." Why? Because the first one to the Fleet Trainer Hangar will also be the first one into the Trainer's pilot seat. Ibanez, of course, wins the race.

"I love the way the *ST* script flips the traditional male/female stereotypes," Richards says. "Carmen acts like the male in a couple's relationship, and Johnny's like a female. I mean, when Carmen leaves for Tereshkova Academy, Rico says 'I love you.' But Carmen won't say that back until Johnny begs her to. Usually it's the other way around."

The full-scale Fleet Trainer into which Carmen and a handful of other cadets then enter was a semi-operational prop. Built primarily of steel, plastic, and wood, and weigh-

Carmen and Zander (rear) enter their escape vehicle in the Lifepod Bay as the Rodger Young *begins to break up around them.*

ing nearly two tons (unoccupied), the Fleet Trainer was a boxy shuttlecraft-type ship built under the aegis (as were all full-scale *ST* vehicles) of construction coordinator Stacey McIntosh and general construction foreman Karen Higgins.

However, the practical effects required to show the full-scale Trainer blasting out of its hangar were under the supervision of John Richardson. "That was done by a very simple endless-cable rig system attached to a forklift waiting outside the set," Richardson says. "The forklift just drove backward and forward; if it moved forward, the Fleet Trainer moved forward, and so on." Twin steel rails roughly sixty feet in length supported the Trainer on its egress from the hangar bay set. Practical sparks and CO_2 blasts supplied by Richardson's department were then shot through the full-scale Trainer's engine exhausts to suggest it's propulsion system was firing up; the live-action engine effects were later enhanced by digitally-created glows and flames laid in by Peter Kuran's Visual Concepts Engineering company.

The 1st Unit ST crew discusses an upcoming Lifepod scene on the small (two-axis) gimbal, used to shake full-scale props placed upon it.

The Small Gimbal

Close-up shots showing Carmen within the cockpit of this Trainer, were filmed on Stage 29, using one of the more unique pieces of live-action equipment acquired for *Starship Troopers*—"the small gimbal."

"A gimbal is essentially an extremely sturdy piece of hydraulically operated equipment which allows any kind of set you've placed on top of it to move in different directions. Up and down, side to side, and so on," explains John Richardson. "Some directors, for example, will build the interior of a submarine or an airliner on a gimbal. They'll then use that to tilt those sets so it looks like the plane's falling out of the sky, or the sub's surfacing from under the ocean."

ST's Fleet Trainer cockpit shots used a "small" gimbal rented from Warner Bros. Studio, upon which the full-scale Trainer cockpit set was placed. Nine feet high, constructed of solid steel, topped by an extendable steel-framed wooden platform measuring 18 by 12 feet, *ST*'s small gimbal was capable of two axes of movement and could slant any set placed upon it up to a maximum 27 degree tilt. The entire rig was hydraulically powered and controlled by two "manual-move" joysticks operated by Richardson team-member Wes Mattox. *ST*'s small gimbal was also not only used for certain Fleet Trainer scenes; further shots featuring the full-scale retrieval boat and lifepod utilized the rocking-and-rolling capabilities of the small gimbal as well.

The *Rodger Young*

Carmen's journey comes to a spectacular end as her Fleet Trainer exits the Lunar Ring and gives audiences their first glimpse of the gigantic battle cruiser *Rodger Young* (a miniature F/X shot courtesy of ILM).

"For the spacecraft seen in *Starship Troopers,*" comments Paul Verhoeven, "I tried to come up with things that would maybe look a little more like what you would think real spaceships in the future could be. Ships like the *Rodger Young*, for example, are not extravagantly streamlined. They wouldn't be, since such craft are moving in space. Every bit of streamlining would be nonsense; there is no air or water resistance in space. So you could say that one of the crucial concepts for the spacecraft we came up with in this picture was 'anti-streamlining.'

"What we tried to do in *ST* was to show audiences ships built in space, strictly for use in space. We also based our ship's designs a little bit on the compact combat planes that were made in the Second World War, like the British Mosquitos."

The bridge of the *Rodger Young* was the most complicated spacecraft control center built for *Starship Troopers*. Approximately twenty feet across and forty feet long, the bridge had numerous functioning "command stations" (for weapons, navigation, engineering, etc.) detailed with winking lights, crew seats, and computer keypads. A revolving central pillar dominating the center of this set (affectionately dubbed "The Nuclear Johnson" by certain male members of the crew) was liberally detailed with DANGER and RADIATION signs, and meant to represent the onboard atomic power source for a rotating communications tower. Mounted dead center on this set was the captain's chair; immediately below and in front of this were the pilot's stations, twin seats which looked out upon a huge, wrap-around "windshield" made from Plexiglas.

Director Paul Verhoeven on location in Hell's Half-Acre, Wyoming.

The Digital Greenscreen

"A really, really important factor in getting the live-action spacecraft shots, especially the bridge on the *Rodger Young*, to perfectly match up with the computer and model effects Sony Pictures Imageworks was going to shoot later, was this device called a digital greenscreen," offers Ernie Farino, SPI's visual effects project producer for *Starship Troopers*. "That used these huge swatches of a stretchy, velour-type fabric that was draped three-quarters of the way around the outside of the bridge and many other sets. These special four- and eight-foot-long fluorescent tubes were then installed under that fabric, and turned on to make it glow. When the camera filmed through the windscreen inside the bridge, it captured this green glowing fabric outside the ship; onto that greenish field we later composited our miniature spacecraft, planets, and starfield footage."

Asteroid, Dead Ahead!

"Impressive" certainly describes a massive piece of filmmaking hardware specifically constructed for the *Rodger Young*/asteroid collision scenes: John Richardson's large gimbal.

"The small gimbal, which we'd rented, was mostly used to give on-stage movement to the smaller spaceship props: the Fleet Trainer, Retreival Boat, and Lifepod," explains Richardson. "But the *Rodger Young* bridge was so big, and some of the scenes it was to be involved with called for such aggressive tilting and shaking of the entire set, that the decision was made to let us build a large, single-axis gimbal onto which that entire set could rest."

Richardson's single-axis gimbal (designed by *ST*'s special effects department head himself) was indeed large. Primarily made of steel, the large gimbal measured forty by fifty feet, weighed twenty thousand pounds, and could support another sixty thousand pounds' worth of sets, actors, technicians and equipment at any one time. It was hinged at one end and resembled a flat, six-foot-high metal platform resting on the soundstage floor. A significant section of this platform could be made to tilt upward toward the Stage 29 ceiling—lifting whatever was placed upon it as well, at a 20 degree angle—by a complex arrangement of vertical rams, pulleys and thick wire cables, which were connected to two steel towers bolted into the concrete floor on either side of the bridge set itself. These lifting movements, in turn, were manipulated by an electronic joystick connected to a computer control system.

"The mechanical advantage of building a set on such a device," Richardson points out, "was that it could lift up the whole front end of the *Rodger Young* bridge about twenty-five feet into the air in five or six seconds. And, by careful operation, it could do some severe jerking of that set at the same time."

Boss Film Studios visual effects supervisor Dave Jones (seated on ladder) contemplates the twenty-foot-long asteroid section built by Boss for that sequence when the Rodger Young *attempts to avoid a collision with an asteroid by diving under it. The back-ground orange fabric—called a "tangerine screen"—will later be used to matte special effects footage into the shot.*

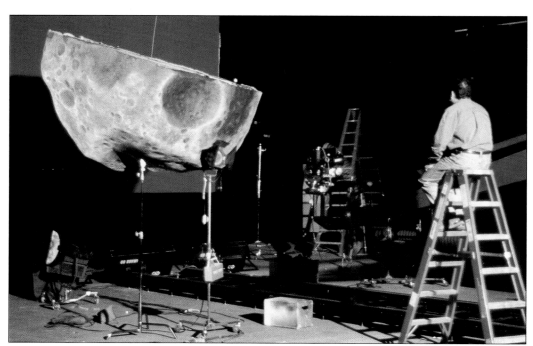

"The dramatic advantage of the large gimbal," adds Alex Funke, SPI project F/X supervisor/director of model photography, "was that all the dynamics of the people being tossed around inside the two sets built upon it—the *Rodger Young* bridge and Lifepod Bay sets—were real dynamics. In other words, by using the single axis gimbal, when a shot called for actors being thrown around because of an asteroid collision or Bug Plasma hits or the *Rodger Young* breaking up, those people actually *were* being thrown around. Their body mass was going where it was being forced to go."

"Both the large and small gimbals were mechanically amazing," concludes Denise Richards, "and very helpful to the cast. We didn't have to lean to one side or pretend we were being thrown around like they did on the *Enterprise* in the old *Star Trek* TV shows, you know? The gimbals did that all for us. Even when we were sitting down, once they tilted those things up or started jerking them around, we really had to fight for our balance. Sometimes we lost it!"

The gimbals also helped capture such gravity-defying shots as the moment when Carmen's cup of hot coffee slowly tilts upward toward one side of its encasing mug, while the rest of the *Rodger Young* bridge remains stable This live-action optical illusion was filmed on the small gimbal as a closeup/insert. The motion picture camera, a small section of Carmen's instrument panel, and a full cup of coffee were each securely fastened to the gimbal itself, which was then tipped to one side. As only the coffee itself moved, the resulting image suggested that the liquid was

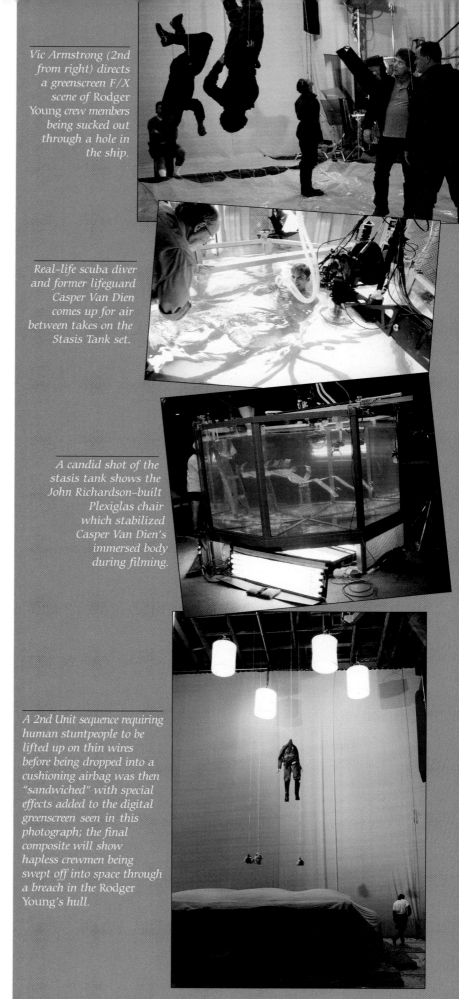

Vic Armstrong (2nd from right) directs a greenscreen F/X scene of Rodger Young crew members being sucked out through a hole in the ship.

Real-life scuba diver and former lifeguard Casper Van Dien comes up for air between takes on the Stasis Tank set.

A candid shot of the stasis tank shows the John Richardson–built Plexiglas chair which stabilized Casper Van Dien's immersed body during filming.

A 2nd Unit sequence requiring human stuntpeople to be lifted up on thin wires before being dropped into a cushioning airbag was then "sandwiched" with special effects added to the digital greenscreen seen in this photograph; the final composite will show hapless crewmen being swept off into space through a breach in the Rodger Young's hull.

being pulled by the gravitational influence of the oncoming asteroid.

"What I have tried to do in *Starship Troopers* is give the ships a little more weight and realism," Verhoeven says. "The way our ships maneuver and move in space, or the way they hit each other and bore themselves into each other during accidental collisions, suggests great, ponderous masses of machinery. You will not see fancy explosions vaporizing ships during the battle scenes, either," the director concludes. "I really tried to avoid the visual cliche of spacecraft being engulfed by explosions; *Pffft!*—they're gone. All these ideas, will, I think, be best shown during the final destruction of the *Rodger Young*, which of course takes place later in the movie."

Fistfight on the Rec Deck

Johnny Rico is ready for battle. "Kill 'em all!" he growls, but his bloodthirsty comment is interrupted by a voice calling his name. It's Carmen, outfitted in a Fleet uniform. Then a slightly drunken Zander arrives—and makes the mistake of challenging the angry Rico to a fistfight inside the *Ticonderoga* battle station.

"The punch-up between Johnny and Zander is a pretty vicious one—but we didn't use any doubles for that," says Dickey Beer, who coordinated the 1st Unit stunts under Vic Armstrong. "The actors did that whole fight all by themselves.

"First I worked out a routine with a couple of stunt men," Beer continues. "Then I videotaped that, had it approved by Paul Verhoeven, and showed the video to Casper Van Dien and Patrick Muldoon. Next the actors rehearsed the moves on that tape, while I taught them how to do stunt-type punches and falls. Finally, I made sure Casper was padded under his uniform, because Zander flips Rico onto this table-top. I had Patrick wear elbow pads, too, because he had to sweep all this stuff off that table. Then Paul Verhoeven said 'Roll it,' and the actors just went at it! No one was hurt; they're both athletic kids. And though it's a serious scene, Casper and Patrick had a lot of fun doing it. In fact, they had a ball!"

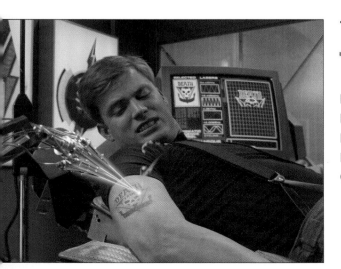

The Tattoo Parlor

"After Johnny and Zander are pulled apart from their fight, Rico and his pals get a laser-tattoo at this parlor on the Rec Deck," continues first unit *ST* makeup artist Bill Meyer. "The Art Department designed those tattoos; they have the words 'Death From Above' printed around a flaming skull. Four actors—Casper, Jake, Dina, Matt—got to wear them. But they weren't genuine tattoos. Those are what's called 'alcohol transfers'; inked, silkscreened designs done on paper backings. To apply that, an alcohol-saturated pad is first put behind that transfer. It soaks through the paper and transfers the outline of the 'tattoo' to the skin. Then you fill in that outline with colored, skin-safe, alcohol-based inks." Computer-generated "tattooing rays" seen burning into Rico's arm were later added by Visual Concepts Engineering during postproduction.

Approximately 50 *ST* "Death From Above" alcohol-transfers were manufactured for the film by Reel Creations, a Los Angeles-based makeup company run by Fred Blau, one specializing in filmic tattoos which has supplied "skin illustrations" for everything from *The Illustrated Man* to *Blade Runner*.

The Drop Ships

Before invading Klendathu, Rico and company secure themselves in a Drop Ship. The sequence, which includes the command-barking Lt. Willy (Steven Ford) ordering Troopers to "kill anything with more than two legs," was filmed in a full-scale, self-enclosed Drop Ship set at Sony Studio's Stage 12. "When you're inside that Ship and see all the Troopers being shaken around by their entry into Klendathu's atmosphere," notes John Richardson, "that's because we actually built that entire set on top of very large, truck-tire inner tubes. Then we attached big vibrator motors onto that set to shake it around, plus three pneumatic rams, to give it violent jerks. All of this made for quite a bumpy ride."

Bug Plasma!

"The Bug Plasma, which is this bluish-white mass of energy that you first see on Klendathu being generated organically by the Plasma Bugs, was all done digitally," explains Sony Imageworks senior visual effects supervisor Scott Anderson. "Tippett Studio did the early development of the Bug Plasma using particle system software, then did a lot of work with the shots showing that plasma leaving the Bugs' bodies. But once it's sort of free of the atmosphere, the Bug Plasma was an effect Sony Imageworks did."

Nuking the Plasma Bugs

Once Rico's Drop Ship lands on Klendathu, Johnny and his friends race up a gentle slope to come face-to-face with two Plasma Bugs. These awesome, eighty-foot high morphologically altered Tanker Bugs are capable of generating tremendous chemical chain reactions within their bodies, and then squirting the resulting substances into space.

After watching the Plasma Bugs discharge their biological weapons into Klendathu's atmosphere (Tippett Studio CG F/X), Rico and Ace respond by firing small, "clean" nuclear missiles at them bazooka-style (these "tactical nuke launchers" were modeled after 1940s-era German Panzer tank Faust missile launchers). The nukes then explode in a blaze of white-hot radioactive light (another Tippett CG effect).

ST producer Jon Davison as he appears in his cameo as the "angry survivor" of the destruction of Buenos Aires. Note the dead (prop) dog.

Shujumi Dies

The invading mobile infantry find themselves overwhelmed by the superior numbers of the defending Bugs. First Lt. Willy is skewered by a marauding Warrior (in a Tippett-created digital effect); then Shujumi suffers a horrendous demise. He is literally torn apart, his hapless body parts flying through the air above a group of attacking Warriors.

Shujumi's final dismemberment was another Tippett CG effect, as was an earlier shot of this Trooper having one leg snipped off. However, the shot leading up to the amputation was done practically. A one-legged stuntman doubling for Anthony Ruivivar was attached to a harness and hung upside-down from the jaws of a sophisticated, full-scale Warrior Bug built by ADI named "MechWar," which featured a completely functional body and head. "The guy doubling for Shujumi was then shaken so violently by MechWar that the stuntman got nauseous," recalls ADI creature animatronics supervisor Yuri Everson. "But he didn't want to spoil the take. So instead of getting sick, that stuntman actually swallowed before he threw up. Upside down, too. That's dedication!"

Katrina's Pit

Panicked by the rapidly escalating chaos around her, Katrina (Blake Lindsley) nervously suggests a hasty retreat just before the ground collapses beneath her feet. She then tumbles into a "Bug Hole" and is dragged from sight by a subterranean Warrior. This scene required careful integration of separate bits of footage: stuntwoman Donna Evans falling into a specially prepared hole dug at the Hell's Half-Acre/Klendathu location, actress Lindsley being pulled out of frame, months later, by a hidden rope running through the bottom of an elaborate, 16-by-12-foot set built on a Sony soundstage called "Katrina's Pit," and a Tippett-created CG Warrior Bug.

Death of a Net Correspondent—and a Kitten

Following Katrina's disappearance down the Bug Hole, a FedNet Correspondent who interviewed Rico onboard the *Ticonderoga* is cut in half by a Warrior Bug's "attack claws" (a completely digital Tippett shot), but not before he is lifted by the full-scale mechanically operated, ADI-constructed Warrior prop (this one a head-only version nicknamed "Snappy").

Next, Kitten Smith (Matt Levin) is ripped to shreds. The attacking Bugs then heave the unfortunate Cap Trooper's *still-living* head, shoulders and arm back at the retreating Rico! This last effect involved a queasily realistic "Kitten dummy," whose head, arm and shoulders were molded from actor Matt Levin by Kevin Yagher Productions.

"Then Yagher Productions, ADI, and Tippett Studio all worked together on that shot where Rico's thigh is impaled by a Warrior's upper jaw at the end of the Klendathu battle sequence," says ADI's Tom Woodruff. "First ADI cast up a full-scale fiberglass replica of a Warrior Bug's upper jaw with its tip cut off. We then physically slammed that jaw down on Casper Van Dien's thigh during filming. Tippet Studio later added a computer-generated jaw tip going into and out of Johnny's leg. And Kevin Yagher's group put a makeup appliance on Casper's leg that was used when Rico pulls that jaw out of his thigh."

The Stasis Tank

The Battle of Klendathu ends with Carmen, onboard the *Ticonderoga*, finding Rico's name on a "Killed in Action" list. Grieving over his apparent death, the young woman "closes" *ST*'s first romantic triangle by allowing Zander to make love to her. Johnny Rico, however, is very much alive. A quick cut reveals him suspended in a liquid-filled "Stasis Tank," an automated medical device patiently healing his wounded thigh through the mechanical application of synthetic flesh.

Approximately ten-feet across, holding 1,200 gallons of specially pH-balanced water, and weighing about six tons filled, the Stasis Tank was made from iron and Plexiglas constructed by John Richardson's group. The automated "knitting machine" seen busily weaving over Rico's thigh was also built by Richardson, who likewise contributed a transparent Plexiglas support to hold Van Dien steadily under water during these shots; this support had been cast off the back half of Van Dien's entire body, and became nearly invisible when submerged in water.

Sugar Watkins

With Rico healed and ready for action, Johnny, Ace, and Dizzy are assigned to a new military unit preparing to mount an assault on the Bug-infested planet of Tango Urilla. Among the first Cap Troopers Johnny and his friends meet in this unit is an intense, bald young warrior proudly wearing part of a Bug Attack Claw as a "trophy" around his neck. This is Sugar Watkins, played by Seth Gilliam.

"The kind of character I saw Sugar Watkins in *Starship Troopers* as being," Gilliam says, "was like the Vietnam veteran who kept reenlisting after every tour of duty was over. To my mind, Sugar couldn't deal with being 'back in the world,' as they used to call it."

Rasczak's Roughnecks

Ace, Rico, and Dizzy are surprised to discover that the name of their new outfit is "Rasczak's Roughnecks" and that their new commanding officer is old friend Jean

*Edward Neumeier, ST's
screenwriter/co-producer,
is a condemned criminal
buttressed by guards.*

Rasczak, who has reenlisted in the Mobile Infantry following the destruction of Buenos Aires. "Rasczak now wears a grey mechanical hand over his stump," notes Kevin Yagher. "That prosthetic was made the same way as the blue metal hand the recruiting officer wore earlier in the film; it's essentially a sculpted and painted urethane foam glove."

Besides a new hand, Rasczak's former students note a change in their former teacher's attitude. Ironside now grimly informs his new Troopers that "I only have one rule. Everyone fights. No one quits. If you don't do your job, I'll shoot you."

"The destruction of Buenos Aires caused a personal tragedy for Rasczak," explains Michael Ironside. "After his family was destroyed along with that city, there isn't a God in Rasczak's life anymore. That makes him a little suicidal."

The Tac Attack

Rasczak tells the Roughnecks that they'll be landing on Tango Urilla as part of a "mop-up operation," once a squadron of Fleet Tactical Fighters carpet-bomb the planet and destroy the majority of the Bugs infesting its surface.

What follows is one of the most spectacular moments in *Starship Troopers*. In a variety of shots combining live-action with post-production special effects, a wedge-shaped formation of Tac Fighters (motion-controlled miniatures filmed by Sony Imageworks, digitally composited into live-action footage filmed at South Dakota's Barber Ranch), unleash death from above.

"The Tac Fighter scene was one of the most incredibly difficult sequences we had to do for the picture," begins Phil Tippett. "You see these huge masses of panicked Warriors trying to escape the futuristic version of a napalm bombing. Hundreds of Bugs and pieces of Bugs are being consumed by fire or thrown up into the air. The digital part of that took a tremendous amount of time and coordination: there were close to a thousand Bugs in a shot, and each one had to be color-balanced, animated and correctly lit, then either vaporized or blown apart. Of course, John Richardson deserves mention too, since he did the explosions themselves. Which were real, and *enormous*."

"I would venture to say that the Tac air strike was one of the largest moving napalm-type runs ever done for a film," Richardson explains. "The final travel distance on those explosions measured 2,500 feet in length; to put it another way, we had a solid sheet of fire nearly *half a mile long*, moving at 300 miles per hour."

Richardson achieved this spectacular effect by first choosing a long, natural valley on Barber Ranch in which to begin his labors. Twenty-eight separate fifty-gallon drums and eight smaller containers were then placed at regular intervals in a half-mile long series of depressions within the valley floor. Each of the drums was turned on its side, sandbagged into place, stuffed with both a high explosive charge and plastic-lined bag of raw gasoline, then left open at one end. When ignited, the burning fuel exited these drums horizontally, helping to suggest the forward motion of the 100-foot fireballs left behind by the Tac Fighters during their bombing run.

Riding the Tanker Bug

Mammoth pyrotechnics aside, the Tango Urilla scenes are chiefly notable for their introduction of the Tanker Bug. This fifty-foot-long, beetle-like, acid-spewing alien is first seen shortly after Dizzy, Rico, and Sugar Watkins have dispatched a number of smaller Warrior Bugs on the planet's surface. Suddenly, the ground under Corporal Birdie's (Ungela Brockman's) unit cracks open, and a massive Tanker Bug crawls to the surface and spews out orange organic acid, immediately melting Birdie's right arm.

The Tanker Bug and acid-spray were Tippett Studio CG F/X, as were shots of Birdie's arm melting. Her resulting stump, however, was a special silicon-based makeup prosthetic, created and applied to Ungela Brockman by Kevin Yagher Productions, Inc.

"Then I ride on the back of the Tanker Bug and blow it up," explains Casper Van Dien. "We shot that in a couple of different stages. First, Dickey Beer, the stunt coordinator, let me jump off a hill onto this tall, narrow wooden scaffolding representing the Tanker Bug's back. Next, I got to literally ride this complicated contraption built by John Richardson and ADI."

ADI had manufactured two 28-foot-long, hand-painted and detailed fiberglass shells which, when joined together, formed a full-scale Tanker Bug back. A twenty-foot long Caterpillar tractor capable of turning on its own axis was then hidden underneath this shell. Tractor and shell were connected together via a complicated, John Richardson–designed network of metal supports, hydraulic rams, and a two-axis gimbal. All this equipment worked in tandem to produce a series of violent, side-to-side and up-and-down movements, suggesting that ADI's "Tanker Bug" was trying to throw Rico to the ground (wide shots showing the entire Tanker Bug violently attempting to shake off the human rider were done digitally by Tippett Studio).

"Actually riding that big plastic shell was a blast," Van Dien concludes. "The whole time, I was about twenty feet up in the air, secured to the shell by a thin piece of piano wire. When that thing thrashed around, man, it *thrashed*. I fell forward. I fell backward. I fell side to side. I did chip a tooth at one point, and bruised my ribs. So what? Even though it was intense, it was worth it. In fact, after we were done, Dickey came up to me and said, "You did a great job. If this acting thing doesn't work out, you always have a job with me." Then he gave me an official Stuntman's Association belt buckle! I was really honored by that."

Hopper Canyon

Following an impromptu nighttime party celebrating their victory over Tango Urilla's Bugs (a sequence actually shot at Vasquez Rocks, CA, following the *ST* company's return to Los Angeles), Dizzy and Rico make love, closing the film's second romantic triangle. One interesting footnote here was the fact that the first night the *Starship Troopers* production company spent filming the Tango Urilla party sequence—Thursday, September 26, 1996—marked the last time in the twentieth century that a total lunar eclipse would be visible from the northern hemisphere.

Rasczak's Roughnecks are now summoned to Planet P—a name taken directly from Heinlein's book—in answer to a mysterious distress call sent by General Owen, from a Mobile Infantry base named Whiskey Outpost. Rasczak's Roughnecks have been chosen to investigate. As the Roughnecks then slowly advance, in formation, down a rocky canyon on Planet P. (a scene filmed on location at Hell's Half-Acre early in *ST*'s shooting

schedule), the canyon itself seems deserted. Its ambiance, however, is tense and foreboding. Moments later, Sergeant Gillespie (Curnal Alesio) becomes another casualty as a winged Hopper Bug glides down from its hiding place in the rocks above and spears Gillespie, carrying the screaming man to a nearby peak.

Colored a beautiful metallic green, the Hoppers, as Phil Tippett explains, "are sort of a genetically-modified cousin to the Warrior

Bugs. They can't really fly, either. What they do is launch themselves from high places and glide on wind currents."

Gillespie's abduction was a combination of practical effects shot live at Hell's Half-Acre by Vic Armstrong's second unit, and of digital effects provided by Tippett's group. The screaming, badly wounded Gillespie is then dropped onto the crags above, where Lt. Rasczak shoots him dead in a mercy killing. "I expect anyone here to do the same for me," Rasczak tells his troops.

The Whiskey Outpost Massacre

The Roughnecks now move out of Hopper Canyon and advance upon the Whiskey Outpost. Situated on a flat, rocky plain dusted with a fine white powder (actually "bentonite," a naturally-occurring substance found at Hell's Half-Acre that is used commercially to lubricate drill bits as they auger their way into the ground), the Whiskey Outpost is a metal-walled compound resembling nothing less than a futuristic Foreign Legion fort.

"That resemblance was intentional," says Paul Verhoeven. "In designing the Whiskey Outpost, we were all thinking of movies like *Beau Geste* (1939), which has a fortress where you can stand on the ramparts behind the walls to defend yourself from an enemy coming at your position from every side. Also, there was a little bit of design influence from the film *Zulu* (1964) which also features a besieged fort, and is one of my favorites."

Climbing up a large ramp into the interior of the Whiskey Outpost, Rasczak's Roughnecks are stunned to see the aftermath of a bloody massacre: dozens of human bodies (and body parts, all polyfoam props by Yagher Productions) are scattered around the interior compound, mingled with the charred and bullet-ridden carcasses of numerous Warriors (full-scale fiberglass Bugs constructed by ADI). A search for survivors yields further mystery—a fifteen-foot-deep hole punched into the floor of the Outpost's Mess Tent (a scene shot on Stage 12 at Sony Pictures Studio). Near this mysterious crater is a strange "Chariot Bug," also dead (this prop, built by Ron Holztheisen of Scientific Arts Studio in Berkeley, CA, was the only life-size *ST* Bug not constructed by ADI).

"Then Rasczak and Dizzy discover a human corpse sitting at a radio in a Communications Tent," continues Kevin Yagher. "Not only does this body have a big hole in the top of its head, its brain's been sucked out. That was a polyfoam dummy we constructed with a fiberglass cavity in its skull. David Barton, one of our guys, then loaded that hole up with ultraslime, bananas, and stage blood. And when Rasczak puts his gloved mechanical hand down inside that hole, and pulls out these chunks of supposed flesh . . . well, it's quite gruesome."

The Second Unit Wraps

Although principal photography was completed on Wednesday, October 16, 1996, nearly six months after the first unit began filming, *Starship Troopers* was far from complete.

For example, Vic Armstrong's second unit continued shooting at Sony Studios exactly one week beyond the first unit's official wrap date. During this period the second unit staged fireball explosions in the Bug Tunnels, captured still more Tippett Bug plates, and, most intriguingly, worked with the "Upside Down Set."

"What happens in this sequence is that during its breakup, a hole opens in the side of the *Rodger Young*, and then exposes the people inside to whatever atmosphere is in that part of space," Armstrong explains. "A few unlucky crew members then fly out of that hole. Much of that will be done as model shots, but the second unit filmed some live-action there as well.

"First, on Stage 29, we built a full-size set representing a crew compartment in the *Rodger Young*. This had flooring, walls, hatchways, a table, and two benches. It stood about thirty-five feet high, and was constructed completely upside down—where the ceiling should have been was the floor, and vice versa. Then we hooked a number of stuntmen and women onto braided steel wires attached to flying belts—hip harnesses worn under their costumes—onto which the wires could be clipped to rotating pivot points. Next we raised these people up to the top of the set and had them turn upside down, to 'sit' on the benches around that table. For the shot itself, we just let gravity take over. The tension on their wires was decreased and the stuntpeople dropped down, still attached to their wires, with their rate of falling controlled by a mechanical safety device I actually invented years and years ago called a 'fan descender.' They landed in a seven-foot-tall air bag. But since the camera filming this was also upside down, the final footage looked as if these people were being sucked *up and out* of the top of the frame."

Starship Troopers' second unit wrapped October 23, 1996. "I thoroughly enjoyed the experience," Armstrong sums up. "Having said that, this still was a long production. *Starship Troopers* had the longest shooting period for a second unit I've ever done—over a hundred-eleven days. But the overall experience was very instructive and constructive, and my crew did some superb stuff. In fact, when people finally go to see the end result, they may not realize it, but at least forty percent of *Starship Troopers* will be second unit work. We did just over nine hundred shots on this picture. Most of them seem to work. I leave a satisfied man."

FedNet Week

Starship Troopers' producers were also generally satisfied with the manner in which *ST*'s principal photography phase had run its course. "Even with all the bad weather, the various illnesses, and the bomb scare, production was not far off from the finishing dates we'd originally penciled in," notes Alan Marshall. "We still wrapped within a competent time frame of what the original schedule was—especially when you take into account our location problems."

"In late October we entered postproduction," continues Jon Davison. "That's a phase when some of a picture's most important elements are added; sound, music, editing, effects."

"A few FedNet and F/X scenes were also filmed during post," adds Alan Marshall. "Originally we had tried to accommodate these sequences during production, by scheduling them for filming by either the first or second units. And while we did indeed shoot a number of FedNet scenes during principal photography, the fact that we were a bit behind caused us not to complete all of them. So we waited until we knew exactly what we wanted, having seen a cut of the film. The studio gave us the ok to shoot the remainder of the FedNet scenes, plus a couple of other little inserts."

Approximately one week of FedNet filming was completed in late January 1997. This footage was not photographed at Sony Studios, however; instead, "FedNet Week" took place mainly on locations in and around Los Angeles.

For example, a FedNet bulletin showing survivors picking through the rubble of Buenos Aires was shot on a vacant lot at the corner of Bay and Wilson Streets in downtown Los Angeles, one which the *ST* crew had carefully detailed with props, broken concrete, and flame effects. Another scene featuring a psychic's "third eye" was shot in a Delta Airlines hangar at Los Angeles International Airport. And during the entire FedNet Week shoot, familiar faces were at work. Paul Verhoeven directed; Jost Vacano handled the photography. More interesting, however, was the fact that a number of *ST* crew members performed *before* the cameras as *actors* during certain FedNet sequences.

Chief among these "crew cameos" was *ST* producer Jon Davison's. He appears as the "Angry Survivor" of the meteor attack on Buenos Aires, informing the camera that "The only good Bug is a dead Bug!" *ST* screenwriter Ed Neumeier was also featured in a

FedNet sequence, as a handcuffed, condemned prisoner standing before three Federation judges at a "Federal Court" (actually a ballroom in downtown LA's Park Plaza Hotel). Moreover, Stacy Lumbrezer, Paul Verhoeven's assistant, was given a close-up in the aforementioned "Psychic" scene as the smiling "Happy Girl."

Even the writer of this book got into the act. Paul M. Sammon appears in a FedNet sequence as a futuristic "Cow Wrangler," pushing a black and white guernsey into a Federation "Bug Pen" just before a captured Warrior Bug tears that unfortunate cow apart (and a CENSORED sign obscures the action).

Months later, the Santa Monica–based Banned From the Ranch company would supply the computer-generated text seen superimposed on various FedNet scenes. But the live-action FedNet Week shoot itself wrapped with minimal fuss.

Unfortunately, another *ST* unit had *not* been operating so smoothly.

The Mobile Infantry land on the alien planet of Klendathu to attack the Bugs.

Crisis with SPI

"One of the major obstacles the *ST* production people had to overcome while they were first making their movie was Sony Pictures Imageworks," reveals a highly placed *Starship* employee. "Originally, Imageworks was supposed to do all the spaceship shots. But for some reason, their presence during most of *ST*'s principal photography was nearly nonexistent. What's ironic about this is that the *ST* people had been forced to accept Imageworks in order to get the movie made!

"Now, Sony Imageworks does employ some nice and talented people. However, it's my opinion that they're poorly managed. So you would have expected the American management or Sony Japan to tell Imageworks to toe the line on this production, since *Starship Troopers* was such a huge studio investment. But that didn't seem to happen. Things were very disorganized from the start on the administrative side of Imageworks for this film."

Rico and a Tanker Bug, which erupts from the ground at Tango Urilla moments before Johnny leaps on its back and blows it to bits. CG insect by Tippett Studio; live-action filmed at the Barber Ranch, South Dakota.

Seeking some possible "whys" for this troublesome situation, the *Starship Troopers* employee goes on to say, "Maybe it was because there was this *other* big science picture shooting at roughly the same time. That was *Contact,* directed by Robert Zemeckis, who did *Forrest Gump.* Imageworks *did* supply F/X for that film. But the Imageworks material for *Starship Troopers* initially got done haphazardly, or not at all. So Big Bug was faced with the situation of having completed a successful production phase, but of knowing that some of the Imageworks F/X were months behind schedule.

"But then, late in production, we were lucky. Laura Buff, our visual effects supervisor, knew of a man working on the Sony lot named Scott Anderson, who'd helped make the

animals talk for *Babe* (1995) and had a good reputation. So Paul Verhoeven then met with Scott. We subsequently insisted that Imageworks make Anderson the SPI F/X supervisor for this picture. Which they did, and he's been great.

   "Scott did a tremendous job," *ST*'s anonymous source continues. But don't think anyone at Big Bug would argue with that, especially since he was hired so late in the game."

Two Troopers flee a Tanker Bug invading the Whiskey Outpost. CG F/X by Tippett Studio.

The eighteen-foot-long Rodger Young *model built by Boss Film Studios hangs from Boss's "overhead motion control" mechanism, aka "the Truss System."*

Still, near the end of 1996, Big Bug reassigned many *ST* special effects shots previously entrusted to Imageworks to a number of other F/X companies. These effects houses included Industrial Light and Magic, Boss Film Corporation, and Mass. Illusion. Why? Because *Starship Troopers* had been originally scheduled for release on July 2, 1997, before being pushed back to July 25. Consequently, to expedite the completion of all effects and to meet these scheduled openings, it was decided to somewhat lighten SPI's load by "jobbing out" certain F/X shots to other companies.

But then TriStar decided to respectively release *Men in Black* on July 2 and *Air Force One* on July 25, instead of *Starship Troopers*. *ST* itself was rescheduled for November 7, 1997. The official reason, according to a TriStar publicist, was "to raise audience awareness regarding the special nature of *ST,* and to bring more people into the theaters."

"Since you don't have an instant name attached to *ST* like Harrison Ford," commented Alan Marshall, "that was probably a sensible idea. Nobody was happy with that decision. We on *ST* felt we'd essentially prepared a summer movie that was now going to be playing in the fall. On the other hand, it might be an advantage. We'll just have to wait and see."

Imageworks FX

Despite the earlier controversies, Sony Pictures Imageworks actually *did* produce a number of excellent segments for *Starship Troopers.* In fact, SPI would shoot over 2,000 separate model elements, utilize 250 employees, and provide approximately 90 *ST* effects shots. But before any of this could happen, certain F/X parameters had to be mapped out, as Scott Anderson explains.

"Generally, we at Imageworks were responsible for developing a lot of the actual physical look of the spacecraft models seen in *ST,* and for the outer space battle sequences. Now, the original spacecraft designs came from production, mostly from a gentleman named Jim Martin, who was an illustrator in the *ST* Art Department. Jim did all the broad strokes, and then Michael Scheffe, who is our art director here at Imageworks, took those elements and sort of digested them down to a somewhat cleaner, striking, and more consistent look. That way all the F/X elements we would be using, on both the digital side and model side, would marry together."

Sony Pictures Imageworks visual effects supervisors Dan Radford, Kelley Ray, senior visual effects supervisor Scott E. Anderson, producer George Merkert and model supervisor Frank Vittori inspect the Rodger Young *model under construction at Thunderstone.*

With ongoing input from director Verhoeven, Imageworks began distinguishing the spaceships seen in *Starship Troopers* from previous celluloid spacecraft through a number of different strategies. One was by assigning three basic "military" colors—blue, tan, and green—to the various Fleet Starships featured in the film. "And Paul Verhoeven suggested," Anderson explains, "that we give the ships massiveness and bulk, something like aircraft carriers or oil tankers. He didn't want small, sleek fighters like you see in *Star Wars.* Instead, the agreement around the model shop was that the *ST* spaceship battle sequences should look more like car chases with supertankers."

Imageworks' miniature spacecraft were built at the Thunderstone Model Shop, a Sony Pictures sister company. Facility supervisor Phil Nataro was in overall charge, while Louis Zutavern was head modelmaker/supervisor and Frank Vittori took on the job description of Thunderstone Model Shop coordinator. Under these men, over a hundred model spacecraft were built for the film. However, many of these miniatures stretched the definition of the word. For example, the largest fully detailed *Rodger Young* model was eighteen feet long, while the largest Retrieval Boat model measured six feet from tip to tip.

ILM model shop technicians ready an exterior portion of the miniature "Lunar Ring Space Station," seen when cadet Carmen Ibanez pilots a Fleet Trainer past and into the Station on a highly exciting ride.

ILM modelmakers detail the full-scale Ticonderoga, *a miniature originally begun by Sony Imageworks and later completed by ILM.*

Photography of the Imageworks miniatures took place at "SIR, a rented commercial stage in Culver City that had exactly the right amount of space we needed for some of *ST*'s bigger model setups," says Alex Funke. This facility was subdivided into three shooting stages, on which all the needed motion-control, stop-motion, and miniature photography could be done. Many of these shots, in turn, were accomplished by computer-controlled cameras mounted on the ends of electronically slaved boom arms, themselves wheeled and running down tracks measuring anywhere from twenty to sixty-five feet in length.

Funke adds, "We also used a couple of huge model movers, or rotating mounts onto which you can attach your miniatures, in conjunction with Imageworks motion-control rigs. These two movers were specifically built for the show by Barry Walton, who's head of engineering at Imageworks. They were assembled at the Sony Imageworks machine shop."

The smaller of these two custom-built model movers could hold miniatures weighing up to fifty pounds and precisely rotate them in varying directions at the same time motion-control photography was under way. The largest mover, however, dubbed "Gigantor" by the Imageworks model photography crew "was really enormous, about the size of a small Toyota truck," Funke continues.

"Gigantor measured about twelve feet across. It's one of, if not the, biggest model movers I've ever seen."

Gigantor's vast mass was needed to support the weight of the heaviest *Rodger Young*-class starship models (of which Imageworks built twenty different versions); some weighed hundreds of pounds. These and other Imageworks miniatures were filmed by Alex Funke and Pete Kozachik (director of model photography). The Imageworks motion control operator was Eric Pascarelli, who in turn was working with SIR stage production manager Don MacBain.

After designing, building, and photographing the many Imageworks models seen in *Starship Troopers,* "everything was digitally composited," explains Scott Anderson. "Various pieces of different elements making up a completed F/X shot—a starfield, a planet, spaceships in orbit above that planet—were pasted together in single frames, frame by frame, by computers. One person who was *incredibly* important to the team there was Dan Radford, the Imageworks CGI visual effects supervisor. Dan not only did a remarkable administrative job, but was exceptionally good in guiding SPI's digital artists and animators."

Other key contributors to Imageworks' digital F/X were Heather Reikels (digital production manager) and "my four CG supervisors," Anderson says. "Their names were Louis Ceterelli, Chad Hammes, Walt Hyneman, and Heather Davis."

One Imageworks digital composite in particular which Anderson thinks reflects

On the SIR/ST model stage in Culver City, two Imageworks miniature technicians study the large "Retrieval Boat" miniature sitting atop SPI's enormous, specially-built model mover (nicknamed "Gigantor").

The Rodger Young *and companions poised in battle over Klendathu. Model and digital effects by SPI.*

Tac Fighters are disgorged from a battle cruiser in high orbit above Tango Urilla. Most of the ships seen here are SPI models. The planet and starfield, however, are the work of Sony Imageworks' digital department.

favorably upon *Starship Troopers* "is that moment about halfway through the film, when the Federal Space Fleet is poised over Klendathu for its invasion. The shot I'm thinking about starts with a close-up of a Drop Ship detatching from the Bull Run starship. Then the camera pans over to show dozens of Fleet ships moving above Klendathu. It's a pretty staggering image. Every type of F/X and scale model we used for *ST* was basically in that one shot.

"There was our eighteen-foot model, which was used for the close-up of the Bull Run when the Drop Ships come off. Later in that shot you see our large-scale Drop Ship minia-

tures, which were about four and a half feet long. We also had one nine-foot-long *Rodger Young*-class and some smaller *Rodger Young*-type ships in the background. All these were then tied in with their sister digital elements; the *Rodger Young*-class ships had digitally added thrusters, the Drop Ships had digital thrusters. Finally, all those ships were flying in a totally digital environment. The stars were digital, the sun, the planet Klendathu, the upcoming Bug plasma; those were also either digitally created or digitally finessed.

"In total, over two hundred separate elements were put together for that single shot," Anderson concludes. "Which is one of the reasons, I think, why scenes like that work so well in the film. You get this feeling of epic claustrophobia by the way Paul Verhoeven decided to drop you right in the middle of the spaceship battles, and those same battles are very detailed, realistic, and exciting. So I really do think that what Imageworks came up with for *Starship Troopers* contains moments that audiences have never seen before—at least not like this!"

ILM FX

Other *ST* effects shots were done by the Marin County-based Industrial Light and Magic, under the guidance of ILM/*ST* visual F/X supervisor Scott Squires, associate VFX supervisor George Murphy, VFX producer Camille Geier, and VFX associate producer Jill Brooks. As Murphy (a six-year ILM veteran who won a Special Effects Oscar for *Forrest Gump*) explains, "The bulk of the material we did for *Starship Troopers* was essentially model and motion-control intensive. Also aggressive—we had only about three months to deliver our shots. That meant we had to have two motion-control crews booked solid and simultaneously for about a hundred and sixty man-days of motion-control shooting, just to get the job done. Marty Rosenberg and Pat Sweeney were in charge of those two crews, but ultimately, we had about eighty ILM people working on our share of the *Starship Troopers* F/X."

ILM's job fundamentally broke down into providing select miniature and digital effects for seven different scenes, among them shots of Dizzy's coffin being launched into space.

To shoot these sequences, ILM first built a number of miniatures, as George Murphy catalogs. "The ILM Model Shop, under Charlie Bailey, constructed a nine-foot-long *Rodger Young* to specs already established by Sony Imageworks, primarily for a number of exterior scenes where you see Carmen undocking the ship from the Lunar Ring and, later, when you get to see a close-up of all this plasma damage the Bugs have wreaked on the ship. The *Rodger Young* docking unit you see on the Lunar Ring was a combination Sony Imageworks/ILM project, a model about six feet across; we detailed it out and added some panelings that connected the dock to the ring itself. Then we built a three-foot-high asteroid, a fifteen-foot-long exterior section of the Lunar Ring, and a motorized gun minia- ture for that opening FedNet shot of an asteroid being blasted to bits by the Lunar Ring gun emplacement. The ILM shop also built a large, fifteen-foot-across-the-top section of the Ticonderoga Battle Station. That's for a scene where you see a few other *Rodger Young*–class ships—which we also built, and were three feet long—limping back home after the Klendathu engagement.

"However," Murphy says, "the other primary *Ticonderoga* model you see in the film was actually sent up to us by Sony Imageworks, who'd already begun building that. This is the minature that shows a full view of the battle station as the *Rodger Young* first approaches it. It's spindle-shaped, and about eight feet high. That model was sort of a work-in-progress; ILM did a lot to finish detailing it."

Under the supervision of CG supervisor David Horsley, digital matte artist Brian Flora, CG animator Jason Ivimey, CG modeler Alyson Markell, and greenscreen/2-D supervisor Tom Rosseter, a host of other ILM computer wizards next contributed various digital F/X to Troopers, mostly using Silicon Graphics computers and available software. These digital tools created a FedNet view of the planet Klendathu and its encircling asteroid belt, a computer-generated coffin and starfield which becomes Dizzy's final resting place, and variously enhanced images of the Earth and its moon. The two massive, snakelike "dock- ing umbilicals" (seen as huge brownish cables connecting the *Rodger Young* to the lunar dock as Carmen backs the ship away from its berth) were also completely computer- generated.

"One ILM sequence I think will be pretty impressive, which involves both miniatures and CG elements," Murphy continues, "is when Carmen flies her Fleet Trainer into and through the interior of the Lunar Ring. We called that 'Carmen's Wild Ride.' Most of those shots featured an incredibly detailed, sixty-foot-long breakaway model tunnel representing the ring's interior. That miniature stood about two feet high. We also ran our motion-control camera through the middle of it, so audiences would feel like they were right in the center of the action.

Dizzy's (Dina Meyer) hand grenade blows the Tanker Bug apart. CG elements by Tippett Studio created the explosion and flying "Bug bits."

"But the Fleet Trainer itself," adds Murphy, "was totally computer-generated during that sequence. The reason we felt we could get away with a CG ship there was because, previously, there'd only been one other moment in *Starship Troopers* where you'd actually gotten to see the Trainer. That was a brief, live-action shot of this full-scale Trainer pulling away from its hangar, which was filmed on a Sony soundstage. Even then you only saw it for a few seconds, so we felt we could go ahead and do the other Fleet Trainer shots as CG elements. Also, this way Paul Verhoeven had the freedom to choreograph the flight of that CG Trainer down the tunnel any way he wanted. And he really took advantage of that freedom—Paul got some dynamic moves going there!"

Boss F/X

While the Northern California-based ILM facility contributed several different *Starship Troopers* sequences, Los Angeles's Boss Film Studios created F/X for only two. But, as Boss visual effects supervisor David Jones points out, both were dazzling.

"Boss contributed about twenty-four shots for *Starship Troopers,* most of which were filmed on two motion-control stages at a place called Syncro Stages, a sort of warehouse at the Van Nuys airport. Besides myself, some of the primary Boss Film folks who contributed to these effects were Jim Rygiel, the other Boss VFX supervisor on this show; our line producer, Gayle Busby; plate line producer, Paige Wilds; our director of photography, Garry Waller; Tim Walker and Derek Prusak, our motion-control operators; and Job Martin, our model shop coordinator.

"What all of us were working toward," continues Jones, "was the successful completion of two sequences involving the *Rodger Young*. The first features a pretty amazing cam-

The Retrieval Boat (model F/X by Sony Imageworks, upper right) lifts off from the overrun Whiskey Outpost, as a Tanker Bug (left, CG by Tippett Studio) sprays it with a blast of computer-generated acid.

era move specified to us by Paul Verhoeven; it begins out in space above the *Rodger Young,* swoops down toward the miniature ship, abruptly tracks off at a ninety-degree angle, swings around, then moves in toward the *Rodger Young*'s bridge, through whose windows you can see Denise Richards. And this all takes place in one shot!"

A swarm of Warrior Bugs attacks the Mobile Infantry.

Boss Film (previous F/X contributor to everything from *Ghostbusters, Die Hard, Species,* and the recent *Air Force One*) achieved this dynamic camera move—known as "Shot IB 1"—through the careful orchestration of numerous disparate elements. Using molds from Sony Imageworks which already incorporated the basic *Rodger Young* model design, Boss first built its own eighteen-foot-long miniature of *ST*'s prime starship. "We then photographed that eighteen-footer as a motion-control shot, using a 24mm Kenworthy snorkel lens attached to the end of a boom arm, for the dive down toward the *Rodger Young* and the subsequent swinging around to the front of the ship," Dave Jones continues.

"That shot was then married to the front end of our *Rodger Young* miniature, which was digitally replaced to make the ship's bow section look more detailed. Finally, that digital section was match-moved to some live-action footage shot by Alex Funke of Denise on the bridge. That had been filmed during principal photography outside the full-scale *Rodger Young* bridge set, with a camera swinging around on a boom. That way all the pieces for this moment could later be invisibly put together for one seamless shot."

However, the most interesting aspect of Boss Film's *Rodger Young* shots was not the ingenuity needed to make an eighteen-foot-long model spaceship appear immense, but the actual manner in which that model was photographed. For Boss did not only use a standard motion-control camera system to film its *Rodger Young* scenes; the effects facility also came up with a novel piece of *equipment* to complement its motion-control work.

"This was a three-point wire system we call the Truss," Dave Jones explains. "What it basically is is a gravity-controlled model mover, a way of hanging a miniature *from the ceiling* of our motion-control stages, somewhat like a giant puppet, and then being able to motion-control the wires holding that model to act in conjunction with our regular computer-controlled camera rigs."

Jones goes on to say that "Two Trusses were custom-built by a guy named Joe Randa and installed at the Syncro Stage just for our *Starship Troopers* effects scenes. Basically, each Truss has three long metal 'fingers' connected to two wired cables each, and is mounted on a track that can run about forty feet back and forth across the ceiling. The whole rig kind of resembles a motion simulator similar to the one that drives the *Star Wars* ride at Disneyland. But ours is turned upside down. And instead of having upright cylinders that work in the normal motion simulator to give you three axes of motion, the Truss has six cables hanging down. By manipulating those wires through software, we could make the *Rodger Young* model bank or turn or rise up and down twelve feet off the deck. The whole time, this enormous model was literally hanging from the ceiling!"

The Truss was also utilized for the second *Starship Troopers* sequence on which Boss Film Studios worked. This involved the *Rodger Young*'s collision with a rogue asteroid. For that sequence, computer-controlled shots of Boss's eighteen-foot-long *Rodger Young* miniature were composited with separately shot footage of a highly detailed, eight-foot-long, Boss-built miniature asteroid. This eight-foot asteroid was then hung from the Truss system and photographed against a tangerine (red) digital effects screen, for use during those moments when the entire asteroid can be seen tumbling toward the starship.

For shots involving the beleaguered ship diving *under* the asteroid to avoid a collision, however, a separate, twenty-foot-long sectional piece of the asteroid was built by the Boss model shop. This was photographed with the motion-controlled Truss system as well.

"But for the moment when that asteroid actually clips off the communications tower of the *Rodger Young*—well, that was done in a totally different way," notes Gayle Busby, Boss's line producer for the *ST* shoot. "First we built a separate model of the communications tower that stood eight feet high and eight feet wide, with a detachable upper section. We then, at night, placed that big model on a runway at the Van Nuys airport. Next we rigged a complicated system of cables, bungee cords, and air cannons to that big miniature, the idea being that those cannons would blast the detachable section along those cables in a controlled flight.

"The final effect looked like this big piece of the tower had been blown off and thrown forward into space," Busby concludes. "Of course, the fact that we set off a big explosion using bags of unleaded gasoline hidden inside that tower at the same time didn't exactly diminish the overall impact either."

VCE F/X

The final company to provide significant special effects to *Starship Troopers* was Visual Concepts Engineering, otherwise known as VCE, and headed by Peter Kuran.

Kuran has been contributing optical, animation, and motion-control effects to the motion picture industry for over twenty years. His first effort of note was animating the optical glows seen around the "light sabres" in *Star Wars*. Since then, Kuran has done everything from providing "Robo Vision" shots for the title character of *RoboCop* to contributing F/X to Oliver Stone's *Nixon* to directing an award-winning documentary on America's nuclear weapons program, titled *Trinity and Beyond: The Atomic Bomb Movie.*

Sergeant Gillespie (Curnal Aulisio) struggles in the lethal clutches of a Hopper Bug.

Troopers manning the ramparts of the Whiskey Outpost fire at the three Phil Tippett–computer-generated Hopper Bugs swooping down on their position.

With the exception of one full-scale Retrieval Boat and a number of full-size Drop Ship Containers—all of which are real—the remainder of the spacecraft and tops of the Drop Ships seen in this shot are actually model spacecraft built, photographed, and composited into live-action Hell's Half-Acre footage by Sony Imageworks.

"But for *Starship Troopers,*" Kuran explains, "VCE acted like a digital utility infielder. That is, we mostly subtracted things or added visual spice. For instance, through computer enhancement we gave more punch to the internal explosions when the *Rodger Young* is breaking up. VCE also digitally removed the wires and platforms that helped Casper Van Dien's stunt-double to do those somersaults during the jumpball game, and matched Jake Busey's real arm to the prosthetic hand Kevin Yagher's group fabricated for the scene where Sergeant Zim pins Ace's hand to a wall with a knife at Camp Currie."

However, working in conjunction with VCE digital supervisor Brian Griffin, effects photographer William Conner, animator Harry Moreau, digital artists Pam Vick and Bryan Cooke, and VCE production coordinator Marilyn Nave, Peter Kuran did more for *Starship Troopers* than merely clean or touch up shots. One important VCE effects assignment involved digitally removing actor Michael Ironside's real arm (which was covered with a gray sock) during *ST*'s opening classroom scene; another was adding dozens of (cel-animated) red, blue, and green laser flashes during the Camp Currie "Laser Tag" and "Live Fire" sequences.

"But I guess the two most high-profile things we did for this picture were the Transporter shots and the scenes where Johnny's leg wound is being healed in the stasis tank," Kuran continues. "VCE's contribution to the first sequence showed Carmen at the Federal Transport Authority building stepping into a Transporter device, which pulls away after its doors close; Carmen is then sucked back into the Transporter network. What we basically did there was, first, get the first unit to shoot a live-action plate of Denise Richards stepping into a full-scale Transporter prop, which was filmed on location at the LA Convention Center. Then Jim Lammers, who did VCE's computer-generated 3-D model work for this show, created a total digital environment around that prop, pulling a perspective change on the live-action footage so that it looked like the capsule was moving backward. Jim also digitally painted in all this stainless-steel tubing around the Transporter capsule as it moved, and so on."

VCE's second contribution to *Starship Troopers* involved Johnny Rico submerged in a "stasis tank," while automated devices painstakingly add synthetic flesh to the Klendathu Bug wound Johnny received in his thigh. This effect was accomplished in two stages. First, Kuran himself supervised the live-action filming of this scene, which was shot with a special motion-control device designed by Joe Lewis, one that boasted a waterproof housing enabling Lewis's computer-controlled camera to repeat precisely controlled moves *underwater.*

Three different setups were then filmed inside the tank with Lewis' rig—one with Casper Van Dien submerged in a prone position, one with nothing in the tank but water, and one with only a Kevin Yagher-constructed prosthetic leg in the tank, a special prop which had been cast off Van Dien's real leg and outfitted with a horrendously deep wound. Months later, VCE composited all three of these elements into a single shot. Digital artist Pam Vick next created a variety of computer-generated "tissue art," after which Vick distorted, manipulated, and added each piece of art on a frame-by-frame basis to the live-action composite. The end result was a suggestion that the stasis tank machinery was actually grafting new skin onto Rico's leg, one layer of tissue at a time.

VCE also added a digitally created tip to the whip which "flogs" Johnny's back, created blue laser beams to burn Rico's "Death from Above" tattoo into his forearm, and inserted a digital camera move onto the close-up of Breckinridge having his head blown off. "All told, we used about fifteen computer workstations for this show," Kuran concludes. "Mostly Macintoshes."

Editing *Starship Troopers*

VCE, ILM, SPI and Boss Film were still not the end of the *Starship Troopers* F/X story. In fact, Mass. Illusion Visual Effects, an East Coast-based company working out of Lenox,

Johnny Rico (foreground) opens fire on a computer–generated Warrior Bug during the Mobile Infantry's mop–up operation on Tango Urilla.

The aftermath of the Bug-directed meteor attack on Buenos Aires. Live-action footage shot in downtown Los Angeles has been enhanced by Mark Sullivan's digital matte painting.

Massachusetts, also contributed many special effects shots to the film, mostly digital composites made up of previously shot SPI elements, although they also built a large-scale model of the Athena starship seen piloted by Captain Carmen Ibanez at *ST*'s end. Further *ST* F/X contributions were made during post by Mark Sullivan, a respected stop-motion animator/matte painter, whose Compound Eye company produced an even dozen digital matte paintings; these included the two moons seen over Hopper Canyon and a painted long shot of "Port Joseph Smith," the Dantana-based Mormon colony devastated by the Bugs.

However, the hard work put into each and every *Starship Troopers* special effects shot still would have been all for nothing had not someone edited that footage into the film. This job fell into the very capable hands of Mark Goldblatt.

Goldblatt is a skilled editor and film buff who "always knew I was going to work in movies; I just wasn't sure how. So I went to a London film school, where I was taught by classic English filmmakers like Wolf Rilla and Clive Donner. When I graduated in 1974, I moved to Hollywood. My first job was as a production assistant—mostly for no pay—on a New World Picture called *Hollywood Boulevard* that was being produced by this guy named Jon Davison."

This shot of Rico's leg wound being healed in a "Stasis Tank" combined live action of Casper Van Dien, a prosthetic leg built by Yagher Productions, and digital imagery supplied by Visual Concepts Engineering.

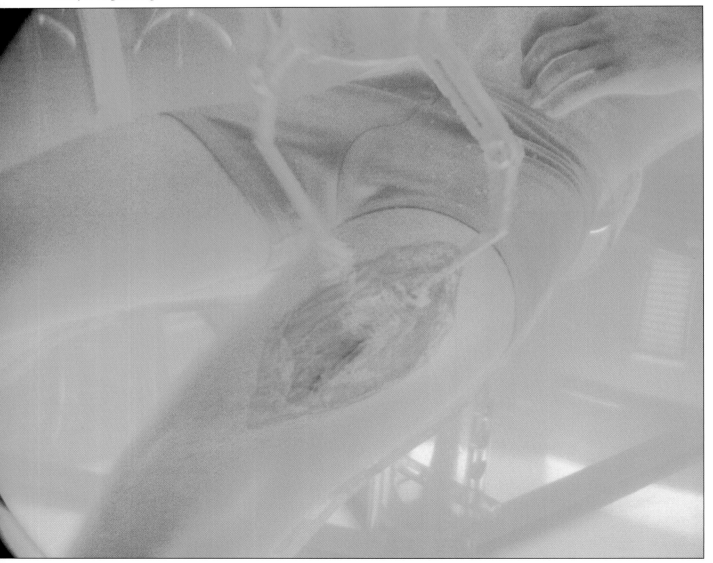

Goldblatt later moved up the filmmaking ladder into the editor's chair, cutting such motion pictures as *The Howling* and *Halloween 2* before being tapped by writer/director James Cameron to edit *The Terminator.* Following the success of that picture, Goldblatt moved onto still higher ground, editing the likes of *Rambo 2, Predator 2, Terminator 2,* and other big-budget action pictures. *ST*'s editor has also *directed* films (like 1989's underrated *The Punisher*) and edited Verhoeven's *Showgirls.*

"My working relationship with Paul Verhoeven is excellent," the bearded editor says. "In fact, Paul recently was a presenter at the American Cinema Editors Awards. And he was very eloquent. He began by talking about editing and how important it was; then Paul said that the job of the director was to interpret the script that the writer provides, while the job of the editor is to interpret the film that the director provides. That's basically been my job on *ST*: to interpret Paul's concept of how the material he's shot from Ed's script might cut together.

"So, having great respect for editing as a process and a craft, Verhoeven basically lets his editors—which was myself and Caroline Ross, in *ST*'s case—cut his film. At the same time, Verhoeven is not one of these people who shoots zillions of feet of footage and hopes that it will later cut together. Instead, like Hitchcock, Paul Verhoeven cuts in the camera. He already knows exactly what he needs. On the other hand, Paul is totally open and receptive to you doing something completely *different* from what his original intentions were.

"Take the visual effects scenes, for example," Goldblatt continues. "Since our visual effects were so complex and groundbreaking, the Bug sequences were among the first shot during production, in order to allow sufficient time to create the shots. Because Paul was completely immersed in shooting six days a week, he encouraged Phil Tippett and I to evaluate the footage and select the best Bug plates, for technical and performance reasons. We would review our selection of plates with Paul on Sundays and then I would edit the sequences and present them to Paul the following week. Phil would also collaborate on these meetings, so that we could lock the sequences in a timely fashion and Phil could go to work on the Bugs.

"I also had some input into suggesting how certain other special effects shots—how a spaceship might move in the frame of a specific setup, for example—should be done before they were actually filmed," Goldblatt footnotes. "In those cases, my advice was mainly based on how a special effect should be shot, so that it would cut in well with the shot before and after it."

Goldblatt's fellow *ST* editorial colleagues were co-editor Caroline Ross, first assistant editor Ian Slater, visual effects editors Julie Webb and Brigitte Daloin, assistant editors Jeff Ervin and Tim Amyx, and apprentice editor Charlotte Spencer. "And they've done a remarkable job," Goldblatt points out.

Yet Goldblatt also realizes that, with a controversial artist like Paul Verhoeven, some of the more provocative *ST* material he has taken pains to splice together may wind up on the cutting room floor.

"Cutting an action film is like doing an action painting," continues Goldblatt. "It's more instinctual than intellectual. And Paul Verhoeven's action sequences are extremely visceral and hard-edged, as befits such a dynamic film artist. He pulls no punches. So when a violent moment occurs, say during a Bug attack, Paul will allow the viewer to experience

Enthusiastic citizens applaud the decision of Sky Marshall Dienes to declare war against the Bugs. This shot incorporates live-action footage shot at both Sony Studio (the podium and stage) and at CalTech (an on-campus auditorium) with a Mark Sullivan matte painting.

*The VCE shot of the
Transporter device
pulling away from
the Federal Transport
Authority building.*

the violence in a very visceral way. Sometimes this approach can result in ratings concerns; i.e., how intense can the film be and still receive an 'R' rating from the MPAA?

"We are very cognizant of such concerns and have been working hard to adhere to MPAA guidelines, without compromising the integrity of our motion picture. But I don't believe we've done anything overly excessive in this picture," Goldblatt concludes. *"Starship Troopers is* a war film, right? And war, as they say, is hell."

The Music

During the *ST* postproduction period, a number of other individuals and companies beyond the Special Effects and Editorial Departments contributed their own important touches to the film. One name in particular stands out—Basil Poledouris.

A multitalented composer and the person responsible for creating some of the most movingly melodic film music to be heard during the past two decades (with his score for 1982's *Conan the Barbarian* a prime example), Poledouris also was responsible for creating the music for *Starship Troopers.* And like many of the other key creative individuals surrounding *ST*'s director, the composer had previously worked with Paul Verhoeven as well, scoring both *Flesh + Blood* and *RoboCop.*

"*ST* is essentially an action movie," Poledouris begins, "an action movie that's unusual in that its characters are fighting against insects. It's also special effects driven—the computer graphics are astounding. So one would think that *ST*'s overall tone is loud and fast.

"Yet Paul Verhoeven actually wants another dimension for the film, which I find commendable. For instance, in particular scenes he goes for a very realistic rendering of what the characters are going through. The death of Dizzy, Carmen's relationship with Johnny and Zander—those sequences are played very straight, and very real. I think Paul expects the same thing of *ST*'s music—which hopefully will not only be exciting, but passionate and poignant."

Part of Poledouris and Verhoeven's strategy for achieving this musical diversity "was to come up with a number of musical leitmotifs, or distinctive themes, for certain characters and protagonists in the show," the composer continues. "That's generally the way Paul likes to work anyway. So there is a musical theme for the Mobile Infantry; a theme for Carmen and Johnny; a theme for Johnny and Dizzy—which is rather crucial, because in a funny sort of way, Dizzy is the real heart of this picture.

"One thing we haven't done, however, is create a full-blooded theme for the most obvious characters in the film—the Bugs. In fact, the way I'm scoring those scenes, the music is almost acting *against* the Bugs. Because the sounds the Bugs make have this incredibly sharp edge. They almost sound electronic, although of course they are organic creatures. So I felt it would be interesting to compose very little music for the Bugs themselves. Instead, I'm primarily scoring the human *reaction* to the Bugs."

Zander (Patrick Muldoon), Johnny (Casper Van Dien) and Carmen (Denise Richards) aboard the Retrieval Boat after the evacuation of the fort.

ST's music, which was heavily dependent on acoustic/percussion instruments and used a full orchestra, was recorded during different sessions on a Sony Studio scoring stage. The largest of these sessions employed ninety-six musicians. *ST* score session dates themselves were from June to September 1997.

Yet it was another, much smaller musical group, one actually appearing in *Starship Troopers* itself, to which Poledouris had the strongest sentimental attachment. "There's a rock band called Evelyn Oz in *ST* that plays during the Prom Dance sequence," Poledouris relates. "That's a real group—my daughter Zoe's, in fact. That's her band. Zoe and Evelyn Oz not only got to appear on camera, they also performed two songs. One's a composition by David Bowie called 'I Have Not Been to Oxford Town.'

"However, the other one—'Born with It'—that's an original. Zoe wrote it. So can you blame a proud father for saying," Poledouris winds up, "that that one song will probably end up being his favorite piece of music in *Starship Troopers*?"

The Tippett Roundup

By late August 1997, the process of creating *ST* was winding down. Approximately four-fifths of the general work entailed in creating a motion picture was complete; the remaining steps primarily involved dubbing, scoring, and editing, three areas which are among the most important "make or break" factors of any motion picture.

But overall, *Starship Troopers* was close enough to completion to generate some final thoughts. One could be, How did the Bugs turn out? After all, it was *ST* producer Jon Davison and director Paul Verhoeven's combined curiosities as to how Phil Tippett would visualize Robert Heinlein's alien insects that had helped generate the movie in the first place.

To answer the question posed above, we turn to Alex Funke, who spoke for the entire production when he said. "Phil, in *Starship Troopers*, is doing stuff that has never been done before. Nobody has ever attempted a movie with over two hundred computer-generated shots at this moment in time, of bugs or anything else, that are completely photorealistic. Phil is breaking totally new ground here.

"I mean, the complicated work Tippett Studio did on the Bugs—their weight, movements, coloration, shadowing, the complex interactions of their surface reflections to the environments around them—is amazing. So this is a gigantic step forward in animation and filmmaking," Funke concludes. "Phil's work is absolutely a window to the future. Not so much because of the particular success of the Bugs in a movie called *Starship Troopers,* but because of the more important fact that *Starship Troopers* and the Bugs have proven that such work can be *done*."

Tippett himself takes such accolades modestly.

"It's nice to be singled out for praise. But the truth is that technical advances are usually a cooperative process. And the Bugs on *Starship Troopers* were definitely a collaborative effort. So many people at Tippett Studio had their hands in making those arachnids sing.

"For instance," Tippett continues, "besides Craig [Hayes] and the other people I've already mentioned, Brennan Doyle, the lead compositor, was very important to this show. As was Joanne Ladolcetta, the lead rotoscoper, and two animators named Pete Konig and Jeremy Cantor and their boss, Trey Stokes, who was the Animation Department head. And

David Rosenthall, the in-and-out supervisor. Then there was Julie Newdoll, who supervised the CG lighting, and Alonzo Ruvalcalba, who helped produce all of the Bug shots. The person who gave me the most support, though, was Jules Roman, Tippett Studios executive producer.

"So it's not fair or proper to simply point my way and say, 'There's the guy who did ST's Bugs,'" Tippett emphasizes. "In fact, I think my job on this show is a lot more easily understood if you look at somebody like Bob Fosse [*Cabaret*] who'd get a bunch of dancers up on a stage and start to build routines around them: 'That looks good, this should look like that, quicker here, slower there.' Because what I've just described is choreography. Directorial stuff. That's what I did for the Bugs of *Starship Troopers*—direct and choreograph. Along with Paul Verhoeven, of course.

"Having said that," Tippett concludes, with a smile, "the Bugs don't look all that bad, do they?"

A bolt of red laser-fire is generated during War Games at Camp Currie; digital special effect by Peter Kuran's Visual Concepts Engineering company.

It's a Wrap

As Paul M. Sammon finishes writing this book, final work on *Starship Troopers* continues to move forward. Not all of the completed special effects had been turned in, the film had not been audience-previewed or locked into an answer print, and *Starship Troopers* has passed with an "R" rating.

Yet even in this relatively unfinished state, *ST* has begun to seek out its audience. The first *Starship Troopers* trailer, for example, was released November 22, 1996, shipped to appear with *Star Trek: First Contact.* Then a second, more dynamic *ST* trailer was placed with the 1997 summer releases *Men in Black* and *Air Force One.* Furthermore, an official *Starship Troopers* Website is already up and running (at *http://www.spe.sony.com/Pictures/SonyMovies/movies/Starship/*), and a "Making of *ST*

BUG SOUND F/X

"*Starship Troopers* Bugs aren't purely fanciful monsters," says sound designer Steve Flick. "They're a realistic, well-thought-out alien race of beetle, grub, and crablike creatures. Consequently, the sounds those Bugs made—their language, if you will—had to be just as realistic and well reasoned."

A longtime film business veteran, Flick is founder and chief of Creative Cafe, an LA-based sound design, editorial, and mixing company. He first worked with *ST's* director and producer in 1985 on that duo's *RoboCop; roughly a decade later, Flick and Creative Cafe were hired to* help give voice to *Starship Troopers'* Bugs.

"John Pospisil, who is a sound designer at Creative Cafe, and I first started working on the Bug sound effects in 1995," Flick continues. "And early on we decided to begin with a unique audio palette. First, whenever possible, we decided to consciously downplay the use of mammalian-based noises for the Bugs. That was only logical, since *ST's* aliens are insects. Next, in 1995, we began actively collecting a whole catalog of interesting natural sound effects. Where we were most fortunate was in hooking up with a fellow at Cornell University named Lang Elliot. Lang's a well-known bird and insect specialist, and he supplied us with a large variety of bug, bird, and frog recordings to use in *Starship Troopers.*

"Creative Cafe then incorporated all of this material with logical conceptual approaches as to why each Bug should sound the way it did," Flick goes on to say. "For instance, you

might notice that there's a drier sound to the Warrior Bugs than there are with the other insects in this picture. Why? Because in the real world a crab is chitinous, and clicks when it walks. Well, the Warriors are supposed to be chitinous as well. So it only followed that they would click too, that the Warriors would sound harder-edged and more arid than the other Bugs."

As Flick explains, the Warrior Bug "voices" themselves were "a diverse palette of bird and insect sounds, including crickets and cockroaches." Yet despite the Warriors' insect-based speech, Flick and his associates did still occasionally opt to use recordings of fur-bearing animals. "One good example of that was the Tanker Bugs," Flick says. "Being much larger than the Warriors, the Tankers demanded a heavier, more lugubrious sound, so by and large we used walrus and seal calls for them. We also used warm-blooded animal noises for the Chariot Bugs; those are the sounds that baby raccoons make when they're suckling. "And of course, most of this audio was then processed by running it through modern electronic technology."

According to Flick, other personnel besides John Pospisil who were important to the creation of *ST's* Bug sounds were "Paul Verhoeven, who's just as creative and involved with sound effects as he is with every other phase of his pictures. Other guys who deserve a lot of praise for the Bug sounds are Kevin O'Connel and Greg Russell, the sound mixers."

CD-ROM" (by ACES Entertainment) had been proposed for the home computer market. Major toy manufacturer Galoob plans a full line of officially licensed *ST* miniatures and action figures, while Dark Horse Comics will release *Insect Touch,* a three-issue *ST* sequel.

Still, the actual experience of making this film—its disappointments and triumphs, hard work and compromises—was rapidly drawing to a close. How, then, did the filmmakers responsible for *Starship Troopers* ultimately feel about their years-long struggle to bring this motion picture to the screen? Alan Marshall is the first to answer:

"This has nothing to do with any artistic issue," Marshall begins. "But, to a certain extent, everything that you work on with the endeavor with which we have worked on this project is worthwhile anyway—whether the film is a huge box-office success or not. On the other hand, one would hate to have been giving this much to a project over a long period of time and then see the project flop. To have *Starship* fall flat on its face would be a disaster!

"Thankfully," Marshall concludes, "right now that scenario seems a dim possibility. Because I think *Starship Troopers* is fine. Better than good, in fact. As something you're proud of, I'm *very* proud of my contribution to this movie."

"Being reunited with the original *RoboCop* creative team was enjoyable and informative," continues Ed Neumeier. "Jon Davison and Paul Verhoeven and, of course, Alan Marshall have really done an unbelievably good job of pulling this movie together. Phil Tippett's Bugs are amazing, too. But you know," Neumeier muses a bit more pensively, "getting any film into production is something of a miracle. So the fact that an influential novel like Robert Heinlein's *Starship Troopers* actually got made into a major movie, and into a film that's such an interesting, groundbreaking movie at that—well, that's just the icing on the cake."

Marshall and Neumeier's final remarks should not be interpreted as the wishful musings of people too close to their own project. The writer of *The Making of Starship Troopers* has now seen close to 80 percent of *Starship Troopers*, and he fully believes that the film's unique blend of futuristic battle scenes, 1950s-era charm, remarkable aliens, character-driven story line, and bittersweet romance will place *Starship Troopers* to the forefront of classic science fiction cinema.

However, lest the reader think that this writer is merely gushing to secure his next writing assignment, ponder this: on Thursday May 29 and Friday May 30, 1997, two rough-cut

Test composite showing various FedNet lettering styles. CG fonts and graphics provided by Banned From the Ranch, Inc.

*Camp Currie, a futuristic
boot camp, was actually
a set built in Fountain
Valley, California's Mile
Square Park. Mark
Sullivan (of Compound
Eye) then expanded
its dimensions by the
addition of a digital
matte painting.*

ST screenings were held for top executives at TriStar and Walt Disney Pictures. Their response? Positive. *Extremely* positive.

So upbeat, in fact, that as I feed these sentences into my word processor, there is already talk of a *Starship* sequel.

Of course, looking back, it's tempting to compare the response of *ST*'s parent studio today with its rather muted puzzlement toward 1994's Bug Test. That irony could turn sardonic if one knew that, years before, an anonymous TriStar "reader" had rated the chances of successfully adapting Heinlein's novel to the screen as only being "fair to poor." In fact, this reader's in-house report (dated July 24, 1991) actually tried to *dissuade* TriStar execs from making *Starship Troopers* in the first place! "With its high budget necessary to create a convincing future and its questionable commercial potential," this memo disdainfully sniffed, "[Heinlein's] novel doesn't offer the thrills or strong lead role to rate further feature consideration."

A critique that only serves to prove the validity of at least one old cliche: "He who laughs last, laughs best."

But the past is past. Despite all odds, *ST* is now posed for a November 7, 1997, debut. A fact which leaves primary *Troopers* participant, Jon Davison, to reflect back on the six long years it took him to bring *Starship Troopers* to the screen.

"Phil Tippett says that making a movie is like being the victim of a violent crime," the producer drolly begins, still hard at work in his Big Bug office, still surrounded by the colorful art that helped launch his latest picture. "You just block it out. But I'll remember *ST* with fondness. I mean that."

"Because at this point in my career," Davison concludes, "I couldn't be happier with the end product. Even with all the ups and downs this project has gone through, *Starship Troopers* is the one production I'm most proud to have my name on."

The final judgment, dear reader, will be yours.

In Wyoming, Paul Verhoeven jogs through the interior of the Whiskey Outpost set while surrounded by a mass of dismembered "background bodies."

P PAUL VERHOEVEN
ON *STARSHIP TROOPERS*

aul Verhoeven was born July 18, 1938, in Amsterdam, Holland. Although he initially attended the University of Leiden for six years with thoughts of becoming a teacher (and, while there, received a Ph.D. in mathematics and physics), Verhoeven's true vocation as a filmmaker manifested itself. His first effort in this area was "A Lizard Too Much" (1960). A short black-and-white film laced with a surrealistic style influenced by Dali, Bunuel, and Resnais, "Lizard" concerned a student who has an affair with two women, one of them married.

Two other shorts—"Let's Have a Party" and "The Wrestler"—followed before Verhoeven entered the Royal Dutch Navy, where he made documentaries like "The Dutch Marine Corps" (1965). This well-shot and kinetically edited short caught the collective eye of the Dutch television industry, which then offered Verhoeven the opportunity to direct after his discharge from the military. One such particularly well-received effort was *Mussert,* a documentary examining the notorious WWII leader of the Dutch Nazi Party who was executed in 1946.

Verhoeven's first major break, however, took place within the realm of historical melodrama. *Floris* (1969) was a children's TV series which became popular with adults as well, and was a fast-paced offering based on the exploits of a legendary figure sometimes called "the Dutch Ivanhoe." *Business Is Business* (1971; aka *Wat Zien Ik*) then became Verhoeven's first commercially released feature film. This was followed by the Dutch-based *Turkish Delight* (an erotic, humorous romance, which established Verhoeven's reputation, and won an Oscar nomination for Best Foreign Language Film of 1973), *Keetje Tippel* (1975; aka *Cathy Tippel; Katie's Passion*), *Soldier of Orange* (1979), *Spetters*, the television film *All Things Pass* and *The Fourth Man*.

Verhoeven's first international coproduction followed with the American/Dutch *Flesh + Blood* (1985). However, it was the 1987 box-office hit *RoboCop*—a dark science fiction satire—that was Verhoeven's first fully American project. *RoboCop* was followed by 1990's *Total Recall* and 1992's *Basic Instinct,* even bigger financial successes. Yet 1995's *Showgirls* earned Verhoeven some of the worst reviews of his career.

It was against this backdrop of controversy that Verhoeven embarked upon his largest, most complex project yet—an adaptation of legendary science fiction writer Robert Heinlein's polemical 1959 novel, *Starship Troopers.*

PAUL SAMMON: Since your current film is based on a well-known book, let's begin by asking what literary science fiction you've read.

PAUL VERHOEVEN: Some, but not much. When I was a kid, I read a lot of Edgar Rice Burroughs's stuff. But for a long time afterward I didn't read any more of it. Until I picked up *Stranger in a Strange Land,* which I got from my brother-in-law when it first came out. *Stranger* was kind of a science fiction best-seller for Robert Heinlein, yes? Then I read, of course, *Dune,* which I highly admired, and later some of Frank Herbert's other works. Plus a lot of other science fiction. Then I stopped reading it altogether, and never picked it up anymore. The reason I stopped was because my interest began slanting much more toward the visualization of things, rather than the reading of books about them.

I know you used to watch a great many American films as a child in The Hague, after World War II. Do you recall seeing any SF films during this period?

Metropolis! That's probably a major influence. Also when I was younger, the first really impressive science fiction movie I saw, that stayed with me for years, including the time that I was drawing, was George Pal's *The War of the Worlds.* And I was always looking at science fiction movies, these B movies from the forties and fifties. Including that one about the giant ants—

Them!

Yes. Jon Davison arranged to show *Them!* to me again, in fact, when I was trying to make up my mind whether to do *Starship Troopers* or not. I watched that film and said, "Yes, there is something here. Maybe I can make these giant bugs work for my own movie." I also liked, as a kid, that one about the giant talking crabs.

Attack of the Crab Monsters?

Yes. Roger Corman. A good little B movie.

I must say that I find that amusing. That Paul Verhoeven, the tough-minded director of Spetters and Basic Instinct, liked Attack of the Crab Monsters.

But it is a kind of classic, no? Remember, I was in my teens and did love this sort of thing. I went to see all these movies. The reading of science fiction, however, has always been a little bit harder for me. I mean, there are too many technical terms and exotic names. Which made the literature a bit too complicated, I thought.

Then what made you pick this particular film to make? After all, Starship Troopers is based on a classic piece of SF literature.

I still like science fiction *movies*. And the script for *Starship Troopers* seemed to promise an extraordinary chance for creating interesting images. That's one reason. I also did this picture for the opportunity to work again with Phil Tippett. I very much enjoyed our experiences together on *RoboCop*.

Did you read Heinlein's original novel to prepare for your film?

No.

Not even a part of it?

A small portion.

Was that decision made so you wouldn't be influenced by the source material?

Yeah. I felt that our own film story was so far away from the book, in a certain way. Because in the novel it is not so much about the insects. It's just more about, let's say, this fascist society, and showing how one becomes a soldier.

I first read Heinlein's novel when I was about twelve, and had fond memories of it. Then, because of my work on this picture, I recently reread Starship Troopers, to find that it had a very strong opening and solid climax. But in between, at least dramatically speaking, there's not much to hang your hat on.

That's basically the way I felt. I read the beginning and thought, "Oh, God, I'm not going to like this." I didn't think there was enough happening in the novel. That the book was just about how people developed their thoughts in this cryptofascist society. On the other hand, I liked that basic concept so much I thought, "That's interesting. That's *very* interesting." So we kept that point of view in the film.

Anyway, I felt it would be better to put my inspiration and ideas into what Ed Neumeier had taken out of the book instead of going back to the source myself. But this is very unusual for me. Normally I read everything.

I had assumed you'd read the entire novel.

No. I purposefully stopped reading *Starship Troopers* after the first forty pages. Because I thought, "This is not the story I want to do."

Forty pages in is about where Johnny Rico gets to boot camp. And the story stops dead.

Yeah, that's why I stopped.

It's the point where Heinlein climbs on his soapbox.

Also the point where I realized I didn't want to do that story.

One of the elements from Heinlein's original novel you did retain was Johnny's flogging.

That was one of the moments I loved, because of its disturbing, suggestive qualities. Also because of its boldness. It was a scene I always wanted in the movie. Would you like to know something humorous? I was cruising the Internet, and found a bunch of comments on *Starship Troopers* by fans of the book who doubted that we would ever do the flogging scene.

We're edging into the social philosophies expounded by Heinlein in his novel, so this seems a good moment to ask how you reacted to the book's conservative elements.

Earlier I used the term "cryptofascism." Perhaps I should say "benign fascism."

Obviously, you witnessed fascism as a child, during the German occupation of your country. So how did a liberal Dutch director who experienced Nazism firsthand react to ST's politics?

Well, I was young during World War II, and didn't exactly know what the political issues of the day were, you know. I was seven when the war ended, and a lot of things happened that I didn't understand. Prior to that, the German presence was more like a military occupation than the fact that I was aware of the Nazi situation. I mean, my parents certainly were. But I couldn't see that at the time.

So I think the essence of my interest in this so-called fascism of Heinlein's, or pseudo-fascism, the real reason I wanted to transfer that to film was that at this moment there are voices in the United States that would actually embrace this form of policy. Which is another reason I wanted to do this film. To carry over the fascist framework from the book to the movie. It's a metaphor, you see—for that part of the American society which would like to have something like the government portrayed in *Starship Troopers* in power in the United States today.

It would also be interesting, I felt, to have the film of *Starship Troopers* make this statement: "This quasi-fascist society we're showing you *works. On a certain level, anyway."*

Is this presentation an endorsement of that alternative?

Well, my point really is, "Do you want this society?" In fact, there's a recurring line in Ed's script which appears during most every FedNet scene; that is, "Would you like to know more?" For Neumeier and myself that meant, "Do you want to know more about this futuristic society?" Or, in another way, what we're asking the audience is, "Do you *like* this society?"

The FedNet scenes are the only third-person glimpses you have into ST's futuristic culture. They also seem to act as a consciously satirical counterpoint to the main narrative.

They are. They are a counterpoint. Still, by seeing and hearing both the scenes in the FedNet and the ones involving the main characters, you get a more dimensional vision of the society they live in. If we had only presented Heinlein's story, straight, I think you would have seen much less of that. You'd think, for instance, during the boot camp scenes, "Wow, that Sergeant Zim is really tough and uncaring. How can he be that way?" But when you see the perspective of the whole society, Zim's character suddenly has depth, and shading. Just as you could also ask yourself, after receiving the perspective of this whole culture, "Would a society that has to fight another race—in this case a nonhuman one—need a dictatorial, or cryptodictatorial, management in order to win?"

Aren't there also parallels between the FedNet sequences in Starship Troopers and the MediaBreak scenes in RoboCop, which served a similarly illuminating function for the fictional culture created for that picture?

Sure. They serve the same purpose. But in *Starship Troopers,* the FedNet scenes are presented in more of a propaganda style. Unlike *RoboCop*'s MediaBreaks, which were basically comedic. Here, the FedNet is more Leni Riefenstahl.

Ah. I'm glad you brought her up. Because in films like Olympiad and Triumph of the Will, Riefenstahl became famous for—among other things—filming large masses of people blocked out in huge geometric configurations. Starship Troopers has its own huge crowd scenes of precisely ordered masses. Which looked a lot like Triumph of the Will to me.

It is. Many of the sequences in *Starship Troopers* featuring the masses of soldiers *are* Leni Riefenstahl. It's just copying from *Triumph of the Will.* In a certain way, of course. In a *free* way. But again, these sequences are also saying, "This is the society we're talking about. Do you like it or not?"

So the "human geometry" crowd scenes in Starship Troopers are your way of visually linking the government of ST's future society to that of the Third Reich's?

In a way. But it's not saying that *ST*'s society is wrong because of that resemblance. It's not making a judgment. These references say, "Here it is. This futuristic society works on this level well—and it fights the giant insects *very* well. Look and decide. The judgment is yours."

Forgive me, but this all sounds a bit disingenuous.

Well, particularly in this film and in *RoboCop,* you are looking upon my own observations about American society, or forces or strong voices in American society. Perhaps not the ultimate voices, hopefully, in American society: but basically strong ones that say to me, with the force of language, what you see in my new movie.

You must realize, however, that such allusions, plus your willingness to carry over the politics of Heinlein's novel, may make your filmed adaptation as controversial as the book.

Of course. But the interesting thing—although, as I said, I haven't read all of Heinlein's book—is that I don't think the film of *Starship Troopers* is a fascist movie. It's not. It's *about* a "sort of" fascist society. Which is different. This returns us to the device of the FedNet, which is an ongoing commentary about this society.

The FedNet sequences do have a certain tongue-in-cheek quality to them which isn't surprising, since all of your films have a certain gleefully audacious undertone.

Right. It's subversive, of course. *Starship Troopers* lures you in and then presents you with the bill, doesn't it? That's what it does.

I just used the word "audacious." The one element in your work which most personally appeals to me is the manner in which you love to push the envelope. Is this a conscious or instinctual preference?

It's probably both. My audacity, as you call it, arises because I sometimes think, "Oh, yeah, I've never seen *that* in a movie!" So I'll do it. Or sometimes you, the audience, basically don't expect me to go further with an idea or an image. But then I do. And sometimes this sense of extremes just comes naturally to me. I mean, it is the images that fill my mind first, you know? Certain times I will think, "Oh, can I do that?" Then I decide, "Sure, fuck it." And I'll go ahead.

At the same time, it seems that your shocking elements are rarely used for purely exploitative effect. Even Basic Instinct's much-publicized sex scenes made sense, in as they appeared in a story about—

Sexual obsession, yeah. Well, it's always the ideas that come first. I see these things, or the writer writes it down, and then looking through the screenplay I suddenly see these images coming up. Anyway, there is a certain extravagance in my treatment of sex and violence in the first place, right? But that's the way I see it.

An interesting aspect of ST is that, unlike the sexuality seen in Showgirls and Basic Instinct, the nudity in Starship Troopers could almost be called "Paul Verhoeven Lite."

Well, that fits the tone of this story. Where *Basic Instinct* was essentially a film about sexual addiction and manipulation, *Troopers,* on one level, is a movie about young romance. The physical act of lovemaking is not an emphasis in this film; it's more spiritual, more idealistic. So my approach to the sex in *Starship Troopers* seemed right for the characters, and for the kind of story we were trying to tell.

Not being Dutch, it's hard for me to make you understand how confused this country is regarding sexual matters.

I don't know if I have discussed this in any other interview, but in a sense I have been referring to this fact all along, and it is something we should acknowledge. That is that I *am* Dutch.

Basically, if you look at Dutch pictorial art in general, and especially when the Dutch made all this wonderful art in the seventeenth century, if you compare these paintings or etchings that were done at that time to art produced in Italy or in Germany or in England or in France, there is a portrayal of reality in Dutch art that is absolutely unique. I mean, I don't think I have seen any other artist except Rembrandt from that period painting or etching a woman who sits on the ground pissing. Which is extremely, let us say, direct. That sense of realism is so unusual, even in the seventeenth century. It's striking how Dutch art reflects somebody being so straight.

So obviously, if you are born in a country with that sort of cultural legacy, I think you are influenced by that. In the sense that it forms you in how you go about observing facts—or in not withholding those facts through your representation of them.

So you're saying your explicitness is essentially a cultural influence.

I think to a large degree, yes. It is also personal, of course. Because not every Dutch guy is doing things the way I do them. They are personal, my interests. But they have also certainly been built up by a society that has had that kind of thinking for a long time.

Moving on to the portrayal of violence in your films, what about your penchant for graphically depicting mutilation, or death? You seem to relish that sort of thing.

Obviously, in war films like *Soldier of Orange,* it is impossible to deal with violence without showing combat situations. As for *Starship Troopers*—well, the animals, the giant Bugs, they split you in two, don't they? Or they stab you with their claws and go right through you. So it's very difficult to be not showing that, the way these animals attack. I like that sort of thing, too, as you just said.

I'm not sure really where that is coming from. Although again, in the seventeenth century, the Dutch excelled in making etchings of torture and painting scenes of people killing each other in the most gruesome way.

The other reason for my preoccupation with violence might be that when I was young, I grew up in an occupied country. I think when your father picks you up in the morning and says, "Let's go to see a plane crash"—I think it was an English plane that was shot down by the Germans and fell not too far from our house—and you go there and see the Germans around that plane picking up pieces of meat and putting them in a little box that was serving as a coffin . . . well, I think that gives you a strange idea, at a very young age, of what physical violence is about. I mean, I was around six at the time this happened. And I remember thinking, "Wow! So that's how it happens! The body is just apart! Well, okay. Now you put it back together again. . . ."

I understand precisely what you mean. My father was in military intelligence and tended to involve me in his work. And when I was around thirteen, I saw a man who'd committed suicide with a service revolver. In my own thirteen-year-old way, this was shocking—but also terribly interesting. Because I'd never seen anyone with the top of their skull erased before. . . .

Right! Exactly! You looked at it like I did! With a very clean, let's say, "neutral" eye. It's part of the world you haven't seen. It's not so different, perhaps, from the stones on the street. Or a glass of water. You think, "Oh, that's there too."

So I think my tolerance for the violent image, in comparison to an American audience's tolerance, might be increased in a certain kind of way. Because some Americans have not been dealing with that, and haven't had the experience of dealing with those images.

This discussion of the graphic depictions of sex and violence in your work usually ends in it being criticized for focusing on the dark, negative side of humanity. Critics say, "Verhoeven's worldview is that everyone is out for themselves. There is no softness or comfort here." Is that actually what you believe?

Yes. Let me put it this way—you cannot say that our century is getting better for people.

It is only getting better in terms of killing. The amount of people that have been killed during the Second World War, or by Stalin, or in Bosnia, or in Indonesia, or in Armenia earlier this century—I mean, look how people behave when they are unhappy over economic circumstances.

Still, despite the darkness and cynicism of your work, have you no belief in love or altruism? I mean, Starship Troopers does end romantically, by reuniting Carmen and Johnny.

Because their other partners are *dead.* Everybody else is killed! I mean, there's only a few people you've gotten to know who are left at the end of this picture. Just about everyone Johnny and Ace got to know in boot camp are dead, Carmen loses everyone on the *Rodger Young* . . . so what does that say about war? And, by extension, mankind in general?

What about the individual? Haven't you encountered specific people who were unselfish, or caring? Haven't you encountered any warmth in your personal life?

Well, yes. I'm not saying individuals are necessarily all bad and think evil thoughts. In fact, I think there are many who do not. So there are individuals who do want to do the good thing. But there are also individuals who want to do the other thing. And the masses vacillate between good and evil. Look how the masses tolerated or endorsed McCarthyism in this country, which was extremely negative. But I'm not denying humanity and goodwill toward people in my work. I'm not denying that at all. I believe goodness exists. Basically I can see it in my nearest companions in life.

So you are right—it is not true that you can put all of humanity in a negative or a positive light. But the negative surely exists. And it is a cruel, powerful force.

You won't hear me arguing against that. Staying with the notion of controversy for a moment, Starship Troopers came under attack—before it was released—by science fiction fans, whose biggest complaint seemed to be your film's exclusion of the powered suits or Power Armor, the mobile exoskeletons which Heinlein created for his novel.

This sort of thing happens all the time with adaptations, and not only science fiction. When *Gone With the Wind* was filmed, for instance, there were the same reactions. "How can you take an English actress like Vivien Leigh and have her portray an American girl from the South?" But it's a different situation when you make a film. One that readers may intellectually understand, but not emotionally. I mean, the book you adapt is catalyzing the process of a film. But it's *not* a film. Or *the* final film.

I heard something on the ST set one day from an actor that's relevant here. He said, "We are not making Robert Heinlein's Starship Troopers. We are making Paul Verhoeven's version of Robert Heinlein's Starship Troopers."

Yes. Or, "Paul Verhoeven's version of a script by Edward Neumeier based on a book by Robert Heinlein." But to specifically address the Power Armor issue, it's not that we didn't try. We did try. I mean, you can see all the Power Armor drawings in the other room. [Verhoeven waves toward producer Jon Davison's office, which is festooned with *ST* conceptual art.] But ultimately we realized we could not work with them. They would not be able to move, really, because they would be so cumbersome. Not to mention expensive.

So, quite simply, I thought it wouldn't work. Well, it *might* work, but that would mean you'd have to put your money there. Anyway, my personal opinion was, I am not making this movie because of Robert Heinlein's Power Suits. I am making this movie because of Phil Tippett and the Bugs. That was the reason I wanted to do this film in the first place. I wanted to work with a highly talented, genius kind of guy. Not because he would make Power Suits for me, but because he would create a new race—a new species, on film.

Power Armor also would have been very expensive, as you've just alluded to. Which is a budget issue. And I don't think science fiction fans or other civilians outside the film industry realize to what an overwhelming extent all films are budget-driven. As opposed to artistically driven.

All of that is true. I certainly didn't have a $100 million special effects budget on this film, that's for sure. If I had, maybe we would have had *lots* of Power Armor.

One of the other major changes you made regarding Heinlein's book involved a sex change for Dizzy Flores. He's a minor male character in the novel but a major female in the film. Why?

In Ed's original outline, Dizzy was also a man, who was only there during the high school scenes. But I felt that it would be more interesting to not only change that character's sex, but to keep her going throughout the story. It was ultimately my sense of realism that saw her as also wanting Johnny. Dizzy wants Johnny, she goes after Johnny, and she gets Johnny. And then she dies. But Johnny is willing to go that way because other things are not going his way. I felt if you could flesh out this Dizzy character, give her and her relationships a more realistic tone, you would have a more interesting human being.

Your portrayals of women in ST seem to have a specific antecedent in RoboCop. Where?

That moment in Robo when the Murphy character, played by Peter Weller, first enters the police station's locker room to change out of his street clothes. A tracking shot reveals seminude women in this locker room who are also changing clothes. But the men take no notice of them. Which I assumed was your way of referring to the fact that the future society of RoboCop promoted a certain gender equality. And that you do, too.

Well, it's very unclear in *RoboCop,* this moment you're referring to, because it is only on the screen for a second. But I understand what you're saying. In that scene, I felt I wanted to visually say, "Okay, what would it be like if men didn't get an erection when there was a naked woman in the background? How would that read? Would that be a more interesting or a bit more pleasant way of looking at things?"

It certainly would be more egalitarian.

Yes. I also have a shower scene in *Starship Troopers* which expands on the locker room sequence in *RoboCop.* This time the women are as foregrounded as the men, have dialogue, and are totally nude. But really, everything is gender-free in *Starship Troopers.* For instance, the top commander of the *Rodger Young* is a woman. Just as the sky marshall is a white male before he fails. Then his position is taken over by a black female.

So this is a personal concern?

Well, yeah. It's kind of trying to be gender-neutral. Based on my strong conviction that women are as strong as men.

Or stronger?

There's no difference in value. That's really my honest feeling. When I was in high school in Holland, there were already mixed-sex classes, because it's a progressive country. And I always felt that the women in my class were as interesting and intelligent as the men. So I really do feel that females are as important as males. And I like to see strong women— as strong as men, as intelligent as men, as resourceful as men.

Speaking of the Dizzy character, what were your feelings concerning Dina Meyer's performance?

Good ones. But the fact is, there really are about half a dozen cast members who are important in this film. Although *Starship Troopers* favors Casper Van Dien, or Johnny, to a certain degree, it still is an ensemble piece. I mean, there are really two female leads who are important, no? Denise Richards and Dina Meyer. Then there is Patrick Muldoon, who plays Zander. And Jake Busey, who is Ace, and . . .

Michael Ironside?

Michael Ironside, and Clancy Brown, and Neil Patrick Harris, of course. So actually you have about eight people who support the framework of the movie. Of course, Casper is the point of the pyramid.

And what Casper specifically brings to the movie as a character—and as a person, in my opinion—is a certain kind of cleanness. Rico is the kind of American boy you would like to have as your own son-in-law. He seems reliable, and strong. He's decent, really. Not opportunistic. Willing to sacrifice himself for major issues. Which is basically a little bit like Casper in real life.

And Denise Richards?

The way the character of Carmen is constructed, you're never exactly sure what she wants or who she wants. *She's* never exactly sure. She is a bit flirtatious to both sides. It is only throughout the movie that she discovers her ultimate choice is Johnny. Still, it's a pretty relative choice, because by then Dina Meyer is dead and Patrick Muldoon is dead. So basically, it's as if circumstances have provided Carmen and Johnny with the conclusion of their lives.

Johnny's much more straight out. He wants Carmen. But when circumstances go against him, he is also willing to go with another woman. Which has a certain realism, right? It's not like the all-too-typical-romantic situation in movies; if circumstances change, the people of *Starship Troopers* change their minds. Or at least are influenced by what's available.

I enjoyed the way ST's opposing romantic triangles spiced the story.

Yes, I felt that it would be just a little bit richer if there were two of these triangles in the film instead of what you would expect from the normal Hollywood movie. Which would be just one.

Frankly, the character elements of Starship Troopers are what most appeal to me. I appreciate the fact that you and Ed Neumeier grafted a human dimension onto a picture that could have been just a series of explosions and effects.

I spent a lot of time and effort trying to avoid that. I always felt that whatever the success of this movie—and success, of course, you cannot foresee—this movie could not and should not be based only on special effects or spaceships—or, especially, on the giant Bugs. In other words, I hoped that the characters would not be wooden and cliched. That they would be real people who want something and don't get it, so they take something else.

Still, despite the realism, what I also find interesting about this picture is that it's an overtly romantic film.

Yes, it is very romantic. But *Starship* also concerns Johnny's love for Carmen, and her being aware . . . of other things than marriage. Career, for example. How she deals with that awareness, and how Rico has to suffer. Because Carmen behaves more "male" than he does. He's not very career-oriented, Johnny Rico. Johnny just wants to be with Carmen.

Which is an inversion of a classic sexual stereotype.

There are a lot of gender reversals in *ST* besides Dizzy's, yes. So the "love" elements in this picture are romantic, and they are not. It's romantic in the way you feel in high school, which I portrayed as having a romantic atmosphere, like during the graduation dance. Even in a school where everyone adheres to a dress code. Which is my comment of what might happen after President Clinton said that we all should have a dress code in high schools, by the way.

How is ST not romantic?

Because it's very realistic in that, as the movie progresses, our main characters, Johnny and Carmen, find, because of circumstances, other partners. That's not very Hollywood, is it? I mean, in normal American movies, our young couple would not be so frustrated in their attempts to romance one another. They also would not normally go off and sleep with other people. Especially in a $100 million American movie!

Virtually every actor on Starship Troopers has spoken quite generously of you. In fact, all the performers I've talked with seemed to love working with you.

I like them, too. I've always liked to work with actors. It's not that I socialize with actors that much in real life, but on the set, I think it's interesting and creative to work closely and at ease with them. I don't agree with Hitchcock's old line about actors being cattle. I'm sure he didn't work with them that way. Maybe sometimes, perhaps, he got pissed off about something. But I think that's part of the fun about filmmaking, working with the actors. And I enjoy working with certain performers more than once. Like Michael Ironside, who was in *Total Recall* and plays Rasczak in this movie. There were also two other people from *Showgirls* here. One is the FedNet reporter (Greg Travis), the other is the girl who plays Birdie (Brockman). She was one of the dancers in *Showgirls,* you know.

On the other hand, none of the performers you've just mentioned could be called big-name stars. In fact, Starship Troopers is one of the biggest-budgeted pictures I can think of without any name value. Yet Hollywood is notoriously talent-driven. Were there any fears that a lack of stars to draw the public in would hurt this picture?

That is certainly true, that there are no big stars in this picture. Although if you look at *Independence Day* and think of that in terms of our movie, there should not be a real problem. Because there were no big stars in that picture either. And there are enough other elements, I think, in this picture as it is to be confident. Of course, if there were also five big stars in this picture, it would be a bit easier. But you have to be practical about these things.

Did you have any problems working with ST's young cast? The majority of them are from episodic television, and had little experience on big-budget theatrical films.

Not really. I mean, sometimes during the first couple of days they had some problems. Some of them were a bit confused, I think. But everyone adapted very well.

I must say I enjoyed watching the very physical way you explain what you want from your actors before a shot. It's quite unusual.

You mean my pantomime?

Your exuberant pantomime. The way you physically act out a performer's movements before a shot. But I have to ask you—American film actors, in particular, are notorious for resenting a director who gets too specific. They seem to think that actors are the only ones who should interpret their parts, whether it be body movements or whatever. Has your approach ever caused any problems?

My approach is sometimes a problem, yes. But on this film, the actors for the most part were very young and inexperienced, so I didn't get as much resistance to my way of showing them what I wanted than I might have gotten from certain older actors.

But I always tell actors before I start my own thing that they should not act it my way, but use whatever I do as information. I'll say, "Don't think that what I'm doing is acting. It's not. Call it ridiculous acting. Or an outside interpretation. But here's a suggestion . . ." Then I yell or wave my arms around or fall to the ground or whatever. What I'm basically trying to communicate is, "Look at me and listen to me before we do the shot. Whatever you think is relevant information in what I'm physically doing or saying, take that into yourself. But you do the acting." I didn't always say that, though. I have learned to do so. Otherwise, people get really offended.

I'm curious: why did you stop making European art films and decide to do Hollywood movies instead?

That's not true.

No?

Not at all—your question is poorly phrased.

In what way?

Because the pictures I did in Holland, with the exception of *The 4th Man,* were not art movies. They were big audience movies. All of them. *Turkish Delight, Keetje Tippel, Soldier of Orange,* all of them. Even *Spetters.* They were all big commercial movies. In fact, Dutch critics hated me because they thought I wasn't artistic enough. Or at all.

That's interesting. Because in this country, since your early films were made in the Netherlands, they were perceived and exhibited as art pictures.

But they were not made that way, and they did not function that way. My scriptwriter and I in Holland— he came from television—we were always trying to make movies that our people, the Dutch people, would understand. For example—*Turkish Delight.* That had more than three million spectators in my country, and the total population is fifteen million.

So in a sense, you haven't changed at all?

No. It looks that way from here, because those films were always considered art films in the USA, as you say. Just as French films are automatically considered art in this country . . . if they ever get here. But in the countries where they are made, foreign pictures are often seen in a very different way.

Let's move on to ST's crew—Dale Dye, for instance. What did you think of the basic-training camp Dye set up for the actors and extras of Starship Troopers before production began?

I think that worked very well. Everybody that had gone with full energy to boot camp did an excellent job during shooting. Dale gave me actors and extras who looked really trained when they came onto the set. So having him aboard was great—although he always protested against our portrayal of the military, of course.

What were your feelings concerning ST's crew in general?

The *Starship Troopers* crew was one of the best I have ever worked with. I think you know me well enough to know I am not just saying that. They were great. Very capable and adult.

I absolutely agree. In fact Starship Troopers, at least during its principal photography phase, was one of the most professionally run shoots it's ever been my pleasure to be associated with.

A lot of that is to be credited to the first assistant director, Gregg Goldstone, and the Second AD, Kenneth Silverstein; I think they both did a great job.

I mention the many storyboards you drew for ST in the preproduction chapter of this book, and how you so rigorously followed them. The boards must have been crucial in successfully finishing the film.

The storyboards were our bible. We had them on the wall of my trailer or sometimes clamped them to a C-stand [*"Century" stand: a metal tripod to which lights are usually attached on the set*]. Then we'd cross off each board as we did them, or an element of them. And we went through them in an absolutely mathematical way. The storyboards were our way of knowing, "Okay, we did this, now we have to go from here to here." That's one reason why we could always work as smoothly and at the pace we did work.

Starship Troopers really was an extraordinarily smooth-running shoot.

I agree with you. This was so well-run, partly because of the people and reasons I have just mentioned. Also, partly because of Alan Marshall being always behind me. That was very important, too. The communication factor was important as well; *Starship Troopers* was a very democratic production. Everybody could bring up ideas, everything could be discussed. I mean, ultimately I had the right to make the final decision, and ultimately I *should* make that decision. Otherwise, if you don't exert that authority and leadership, you're fucked. Somebody has to be driving the bus. Because there is no time to screw around while you're making movies.

Speaking of Alan Marshall . . .

He made my job a lot easier, yes. Alan was very, very important, every day. I wouldn't have started this picture without Alan.

What about Jon Davison? You've worked with him twice, so there must be a certain respect there as well.

Of course. I mean, I think that Jon is the one who coached this film into being at the beginning, right? And Jon set up the whole thing with Phil, basically; I think it was his idea to do the movie with Tippett providing CG Bugs. So, because this movie was so difficult, it was great that we had two producers working on it. They were both terrific, supporting me all the way.

What about the problem with Sony Imageworks? What happened there?

For whatever reasons, when *Starship Troopers* had just first started, my working relationship with Sony Imageworks wasn't very smooth. I just couldn't get a grip on their creative team—perhaps we were on the wrong wavelength.

But then Laura Buff, *ST*'s visual effects producer, told us that a fellow named Scott Anderson, who Phil Tippett knew but I didn't, was working at the studio. Scott had done *Babe* and a number of other special effects films, and Phil spoke highly of him. I then realized that there might be a guy here at Sony who was good enough to do *Starship.* And we were very lucky with Scott—I almost feel like we won the lottery. Because from the moment I started to talk to Scott Anderson and Scott decided to do the movie, the Imageworks effects started to fall into place.

So to sum up, there was a period where nothing happened with Imageworks; nothing fell into place; then Scott took the reins, and everything fell into place. Anderson's been great for this movie. He's extremely precise, deeply committed, a great artist, and a good leader. His group has been coming up with excellent shots.

Which is kind of ironic, yes? Because I always wanted *ST*'s outer space and spaceship effects to be on a par with the Bug F/X. Now, with Scott Anderson's help, they are. Which means I've come full circle on this issue; Imageworks has done astonishing work throughout.

What's your opinion on the special effects contributions of ADI, Kevin Yagher Productions, and Peter Kuran's VCE company?

Excellent. Yagher's, Kuran's, and ADI's work fits seamlessly into the movie. I don't think you can see where it goes from the digital stuff Tippett did to their work. All those groups were extremely committed, and did an excellent job.

I also should mention the fact that, in general, Sony Pictures was very good, very supportive of me. They left me alone and let me make my movie. I very much appreciated that.

We keep returning to Phil Tippett. Let's focus in on him, and then the Bugs.

Well, in fact, Phil was like another director on this picture. Which is a good thing to point out, that there were two directors on this movie. No, wait. There were three. Vic Armstrong, of course, was the third. I mean, Vic did nine hundred shots on *Starship Troopers*! I did twelve hundred, but Vic Armstrong and his crew did nine hundred. While Phil and his crew will be doing about two hundred shots. So there's been *three* directors on this picture, really.

That's another reason I think this shoot went so smoothly. I prepared for it very well, but without Vic and Phil, that preparation would have been nothing. Tippett actually had a great influence on the mechanical process of making this movie as well.

Give me an example.

Well, I like to use the SteadiCam, yes? This floating, sort of handheld camera. Because I think SteadiCam gives a scene a bit more chaos; if it's handheld and not on a dolly, the shot looks a little less arranged, feels a bit more pseudodocumentary, and has more energy. On the other hand, I had to be careful with SteadiCam on this picture. Because to use it during some of the Bug-plate shots meant you were, in effect, making a three-dimensional move. A shot with three axes of movement. And to later put insects into a three-dimensional camera move is extremely complicated, especially for the CGI process. So whenever I could get away with using SteadiCam without Phil protesting that the shot was getting too complicated, I did. That is a very good example of how *Starship Troopers'* "second director" influenced the movie beyond his Bugs.

Another interesting photographic technique, and one which I don't think I've seen used before, was that whenever ST's action switches to an outer space environment, the camera appears to be weightless. Was this intentional?

Yes, absolutely. I wanted to give those outer space scenes another look. What we've all seen before, and it's given us a lot of pleasure, are the *Stars Wars*–type of outer space sequences, where the cutting and F/X moves are very dynamic. But the live-action space sequences, especially, look technically—and, by extension, emotionally—"locked down."

I felt in *Starship Troopers'* case we could try something different. That we could subtly suggest, perhaps, more of a feeling of ships maneuvering at sea. As if a floating camera witnessed these outer space events in a weightless environment, with the camera exhibiting a bit more movement. Like a gyroscope hanging in a weightless room. That was the idea, anyway.

Back to Tippett and the Bugs: How much of the design of these alien insects was yours?

It's all Phil's and Craig Hayes's, his partner. I mean, they discussed this with us, but I cannot claim anything in terms of original design. Yes, there was an ongoing process of refinement, but the ideas were all coming from them. That's why I wanted to work with them! Because I thought there could be something new and different.

Tippett and his coworkers certainly filled the bill there, because Starship Troopers has much more by way of Bugs than the novel does: Warrior Bugs, Tanker Bugs, Chariot Bugs, Plasma Bugs . . .

Right, right . . .

Which, interestingly enough, implies a sort of hierarchy.

Yes. That's one idea we tried to get across. Which was already in the script, in a sense. But Phil's group *made* the Bugs. He and Craig came to us with proposals and all these original drawings—"What about this kind of Bug, what about that?"—years ago, back in 1993. We then discussed it all, of course: "Can you do this, can you change that?" But I cannot claim rights to the Bugs. Heinlein created them first, then Phil Tippett and his people visualized them, in three dimensions. Which made the Bugs the stars of this movie.

On the other hand, the big decision regarding our Bugs was to have a biological as opposed to anthropomorphic presentation of them, so that the Bugs would be like real insects. So that they would not be "thinking" and "reacting" in a human way. The bottom line on the whole Bug issue is that I wanted to do something that could be true on another planet—believable Bugs, with believable biological capabilities and a believable social hierarchy. That's where I decided to focus the budget. Which isn't infinite, you know. Even on a so-called big-budget movie.

Ed Neumeier did tell me that there was a conscious decision to not go with a giant cockroach holding a ray gun.

Yes. I mean, the book says the insects had guns, right? Which I just felt was nonsense—bugs with guns. That's not something I believe would exist in the whole universe. So, you'll never see our Bugs using any technology or instruments; all of their weapons come from their own bodies. The Bugs kill with their jaws or their claws, or acid, or plasma. They're really big, dangerous animals. Still, you can shoot at them. And kill them. Which is also believable.

However, the fact that the biological weapons these Bugs use are so specialized suggests interesting things about their society, right? Which we unfortunately don't see that much of.

What little we do see of the arachnid society in this picture has few, if any, human emotions.

No. But that's how we humans always see our enemy. Demonization is the norm. When we fight a Saddam Hussein, he's immediately the Devil, and the incarnation of evil. All of his citizens are devils, too. That's why the insects are not humanized in this picture. Because in no enemy that you fight a life-and-death battle against will you be able to see anything human anymore.

Yet what I like about the Bugs is that they exhibit a certain character. For instance, the ferocity of the Warriors is very frightening.

Some of them have character. But sometimes this is also just a war movie, you know? Then the Bugs don't have character—they're just a multitude.

Like that "swarm shot" of the Warriors besieging the Whiskey Outpost? Which, I have to tell you, is an amazing sequence.

Incredible, yeah. Like I said, Tippett is a genius kind of guy.

What about the personality of the Brain Bug? It exudes an aura of genuine alien evil.

Exactly. He is an evil god, really. In fact, I always felt the Brain Bug was like a monster out of an H. P. Lovecraft story. Almost like his famous "Chew-loo," with its multiple eyes and whatnot.

Chew-loo? Do you mean Cthulhu, or "Ka-THOO-loo," as I pronounce it? From Lovecraft's novella The Call of Cthulhu?

That's who I mean. We pronounce his name almost like "Chew-chew" in Holland.

I never knew you were a Lovecraft fan.

Oh, yes. I read a lot of Lovecraft when I was in my twenties. And when I was getting the look of the Brain Bug from Tippett and shooting its scenes with the full-scale ADI Brain Bug, I really felt closely connected to Lovecraft. The Brain Bug was like an evil Lovecraftian god to me, one of "The Old Ones." One that was coming out of the darkness of the Bug Tunnels. Coming out of the earth, in fact. Which is a favorite Lovecraftian motif.

I enjoyed the way you staged Zander's confrontation with the Brain Bug. Patrick Muldoon does the standard heroic human thing, literally spits in the Brain Bug's face, but then, SWAK!—he's immediately killed for doing so. Which not only runs contrary to expectation, but also plays as if this human has committed a sacrilege.

Yeah! It is almost a sacrilegious act, to spit in the face of this evil god. Zander is swiftly punished for that.

You mentioned the Bug Tunnels, in which the Brain Bug lives. Did you have anything specifically in mind regarding the design of these habitats?

Not much beyond the obvious. Since we tried to make our insects realistic, I thought you would expect the tunnels to look like they'd been built by real bugs too. Like an ant colony, with all these corridors. Except that our tunnels have been built by much bigger ants. Of course, they aren't ants, these insect Warriors. They're more like arachnids.

Insects or arachnids, during the production of Starship Troopers you were working on a film whose stars were primarily generated by computers. This meant you couldn't see them during principal photography. Was that ever a problem?

Well, it was sometimes frustrating to shoot. Because for all of those sequences, to a large degree, you're shooting effects plates. Shots where the camera is locked down or on a motion-control head, and you're filming people interacting with or shooting at things that aren't there. So you really have to believe in your original concept and original vision to get through those kind of days.

Has it been working so far?

I think so, yeah. Much of the effects stuff in *Starship Troopers* will look interesting and pretty real, I think. The Bugs certainly seem to be integrated into the shots.

We've just about wrapped this up. But since I know how important musical scores are to you, and that at the moment you are working with Basil Poledouris on Starship Troopers' score, can I ask what kind of music you're after on this picture?

The score for *Starship Troopers* needs a military tone, I think. But also maybe a little fascistic, if I can use that word. It should wink a bit toward Wagner. Then again, it should be passionate. Because people *die* in this movie. This isn't one of those comfortable movies where everyone survives.

I can say that on the temp music tracks we have used all kinds of people, from Wagner to Stravinsky to James Horner. So there also might be a lot of drums and horns and brass in *ST*'s music, I think. Maybe a bit like James Horner's score for *Aliens,* Basil's for *Conan the Barbarian.* Both of which I like a lot.

I was happy to hear you were working with Poledouris again, since his music—

—is filled with a lot of soul. Yes. I think that the passion and warmth you hear in Basil's music is because he's that kind of guy. He's not very intellectual. He goes more for an instinct, or type of feeling.

Music from the heart, in other words.

Right, from the heart. *Starship Troopers* is that type of movie, oddly enough. Although there will be all these strange animals and starships, I still think that what will basically touch you in this movie will be the fate of its characters. The ones who don't survive.

Which almost sounds like the perfect place to end this interview—except for one final question. At this point in time, you're about two-thirds of the way through the making of Starship Troopers. My question is, What are your instincts about this picture? Or do you allow yourself the luxury of such thoughts?

Of course I'm thinking about how good or bad this movie is. I'm working on it every day!

Then let me be more specific. How are you personally feeling about Starship Troopers? Right now?

Sometimes I like it, and sometimes I think, "What the fuck did I do?" But that's normal, you know. Because I've never made a movie yet where I felt, "This is great!"

With the exception of Showgirls . . . [smiles].

A Somber Farewell

By late fall 1996, principal photography on *Starship Troopers* was nearing its end. The company had already spent months braving Hell's Half-Acre's bizarre weather, enjoying the relative calm of the Barber Ranch, and methodically moving from set-up to set-up at the Sony Studio and at various locations scattered around Los Angeles. During this time, the *ST* crew had endured floods, snowstorms, heat exhaustion, respiratory illnesses, and the garden-variety exhaustion which goes hand-in-glove with making any motion picture.

Yet this litany of weather-oriented misadventures pales beside the two other events which marked the production's most unfortunate moments.

One occurred just as the company was preparing to leave Wyoming for Los Angeles. At this point, the *ST* filmmakers had already spent six weeks filming in Casper (from April 29 to June 12, 1996). They had then left for South Dakota on June 14 to shoot the Tango Urilla sequences, and returned to Casper on June 26 to complete the end of the Klendathu battle. So when the *ST* company boarded a chartered Los Angeles-bound jet at the Casper airport the evening of June 29, spirits were high. Most of the crew would now be returning to their homes in Los Angeles, where principal photography was set to resume July 3.

Unfortunately, spirits of another kind were seemingly responsible for making sure the company didn't leave Casper that day. An apparently inebriated *ST* crew member, denied further alcohol by the flight attendants while the plane was still on the ground, reportedly muttered something about "getting a drink or having a bomb go off." What was obviously a drunken protest was taken in earnest—the jet's passengers were whisked off to a holding area, and its cargo bay thoroughly searched tor explosives. No bomb was found; however, searched luggage did reveal a number of fireworks (understandable, if not laudable, since the Fourth of July holiday was only days away), plus a small amount of marijuana. Yet despite the absence of any destructive device, the offending crewmember was promptly arrested for violating Federal bomb threat statutes. And the plane's passengers, all *ST* crew members, now spent the better part of twenty-four hours waiting for the legal and bureaucratic processes involved in this incident to resolve themselves to a point where the *ST* crew could once again retum to LA.

"Basicaly, the impact of the bomb threat was that we had to travel on a rest day," remembers Jon Davison. "We also lost a day of shooting back in Los Angeles, which was costly. So what appears to be a drunken prank flew totally out of control. But Alan Marshall straightened everything out."

Alan Marshall can also recall what, sadly, became the single most tragic misfortune to befall *Starship Troopers*.

"During the (1996) Memorial Day weekend, while we were shooting in Wyoming," Marshall begins, "some of the crew had driven to Yellowstone Park to enjoy themselves and forget about the film for a couple of days. About 11 P.M. on the final night of the holiday, a caravan of crew members was making their way back to Casper when a terrible accident happened. Apparently, a car coming from the opposite direction crossed the center line at high speed and crashed head-on into an automobile filled with our people. Two of them— Gavin Gharrity and Tom O'Halloran—were killed instantly. A third passenger, Rachel Campos, who was the girlfriend of Gavin and visiting him for the holidays, was seriously injured. The other driver was also killed.

"I spoke to the Natrona County Coroner later about this—the crash happened only about eighty miles outside of Casper—and, in his opinion, the police would have taken action against the other driver had that other driver survived. Because he had indeed wandered across the center line. And if drugs or alcohol were not involved, which was the rumor, then apparently this other driver had just fallen asleep at the wheel. Which is a double tragedy."

The deaths of these fellow filmmakers deeply affected *ST*'s crew. Psychological counseling was required for some, while Rachel Campos (who had achieved a small measure of fame as a participant in the "Puck" episodes of MTV's youth-oriented reality program *The Real World*) was forced to endure months of convalescence and physical therapy.

"But Disney and TriStar came through for Rachel by making sure that her medical bills, which were substantial, were at least partially paid," Marshall continues. "The *Starship* crew also put in numerous donations; Phil Tippett even had a bunch of T-shirts printed up for sale to the crew, and those profits were turned directly over to Rachel to help cover her medical expenses. So in that sense, Rachel was helped by everyone.

"Yet that accident was still an awful thing," concludes Marshall. "Gavin and Tom's deaths touched the hearts of hundreds and hundreds of people."

About the Author

Since 1972, PAUL M. SAMMON has combined his passions for film and literature by working on motion pictures and writing about them.

The Making of Starship Troopers author Paul M. Sammon meets the Brain Bug.

As a writer, Sammon's latest project was the best-selling *Future Noir: The Making of Blade Runner* (1996). He also edited the controversial "extreme horror" anthologies *Splatterpunks* (1990) and *Splatterpunks II* (1995), authored *The Christmas Carol Trivia Book* (1994), and edited *The King Is Dead*, a 1995 collection of articles, essays, and short stories examining the Elvis Presley phenomenon.

As a filmmaker, Sammon has worked on dozens of motion pictures in numerous capacities. He began in the marketing department of Universal Pictures in 1979; by the mid-80's, Sammon had worked his way up to a position as vice president of special promotions at another major studio. He then went independent. Sammon has since supplied services or "crewed" on such motion pictures as *RoboCop, Blue Velvet, Conan the Barbarian, The Silence of the Lambs*, and *Dune*. He also was computer graphics supervisor for *RoboCop 2*, digital and optical effects supervisor for *Xtro: Watch the Skies,* and has been a still photographer, 2nd unit director, documentary director, and producer (for a number of Japanese TV series).

For *Starship Troopers*, Paul M. Sammon was "on set" nearly every day of the six months it took to film director Paul Verhoeven's adaptation of author Robert A. Heinlein's classic SF novel. Sammon was also present during *ST*'s preproduction and postproduction periods, functioned as a 2nd unit/special effects still photographer, and conducted over 200 interviews for *The Making of ST*.

Paul M. Sammon also *acted* in *Starship Troopers*— alongside a giant Warrior Bug and Sarah the cow.

Immediately after the final shot on the last day of 1st unit photography, ST's cast and crew pose for a group photo on the Bug Tunnels set; "It's a Wrap!"